PRAISE FOR
HAMILTON
BY THE SLICE

"The world loves George Washington, and Washington loved Alexander Hamilton. The reasons stand out loud and clear as you read this insightful book. I recommend *Hamilton by the Slice* to any busy person who wants to understand Hamilton, an extraordinary American Founder who played a pivotal role in shaping the new United States."

> —John Ferling, author of the recently published
> *The Ascent of George Washington: The Hidden*
> *Political Genius of an American Icon*

"If you want to think like a great person, you must know how great people think. Bill Chrystal picks quotes that exemplify how and what this brilliant General (Hamilton) thought about a wide range of subjects. I recommend this to anyone who wants to get ahead in life."

> —Lt. Gen. Samuel V. Wilson, U.S. Army (Ret.),
> President Emeritus, Hampden-Sydney College

"What a daunting task—bringing Hamilton alive with relaxed and conversational authority! Bill Chrystal gives us Hamilton's wisdom and underlying principles in short stand alone chapters, allowing the reader to

pick and choose what he or she wants to know first, then second, etc. This easy-to-read book makes one of the most complex and influential Founding Fathers accessible to a 21st century America. Great piece of work!"
—Patrick Murphrey, M.P.A., President,
Hamilton-Jefferson Society,
Regent University

"This is a fresh approach! Bill Chrystal has written a fun and informative book for the non-historian. Few people know Hamilton well enough to recognize his finger prints in their everyday lives. The topic by topic approach makes it possible to quickly understand and absorb Hamilton's wisdom."
—James F. Pontuso, Patterson Professor
Department of Government & Foreign Affairs,
Hampden-Sydney College

"*Hamilton by the Slice* is history for people on the go! Bill Chrystal has written a concise and insightful account of one of our most important founding fathers. Alexander Hamilton's story is a classic American story, and, for better or worse, we live in the nation he envisioned. Bill Chrystal's book is a passionate reminder of all that we owe to this most farsighted member of the founding generation."
—Stephen F. Knott, author of
Alexander Hamilton and the Persistence of Myth

HAMILTON
BY THE
SLICE

HAMILTON BY THE SLICE

Falling in Love With Our Most Influential Founding Father

— ∾ —

William G. Chrystal

Empire for Liberty, LLC.

Edition ISBNs:
PDF 978-0-9819760-0-6
Audio, MP3 978-0-9819760-1-3

ISBN 978-0-9819760-7-5

Library of Congress Control Number: 2009925267

Printed in Canada
Empire for Liberty, LLC
6015 S. Virginia St.
Suite E, #458
Reno, Nevada 89502

For Marjorie Chrystal

&

Charlie and DJ Guill

CONTENTS

ABOUT THE AUTHOR

William G. (Bill) Chrystal is a first-person historical interpreter of Alexander Hamilton. He brings Hamilton alive for college and university students, library patrons, and business and professional leaders.

Bill is a graduate of the University of Washington and has advanced degrees from the University of Washington, Eden Theological Seminary, and Johns Hopkins University. For thirty years, Bill was a Congregational Minister (United Church of Christ); five were spent as a Navy Chaplain.

Bill is the author and editor of two books on the influential Niebuhr family. He has written for many magazines, newspapers, and scholarly journals, including *The New England Quarterly, Church History,* and *Theology Today.* For more than ten years he was the host of the NPR program, "The Thomas Jefferson Hour."

Currently, he portrays both John Adams and Alexander Hamilton. We invite you to visit his Web sites: *www.HamiltonSpeaks.com, www.BillChrystal.com, and www.JohnAdamsLives.com.*

PREFACE

Alexander Hamilton was born on the British Island of Nevis on January 11, 1757, to James Hamilton and Rachel Faucett Lavien. For years, scholars have discussed and debated two things: whether or not Hamilton's parents were married and what year was Hamilton born.

Let's first explore the question of legitimacy. This is what we know for sure: Rachel left her first husband, Johann Michael Lavien, when they lived on the neighboring island of Saint Croix, a Danish possession. Johann later obtained a divorce and, under Danish law, he was free to remarry but Rachel was not.

Alexander Hamilton said his parents married on the Island of Saint Kitts, a British possession. No records have been found to that effect. However, when Rachel moved with her new family back to Saint Croix in 1765 or 1766, her marriage to James Hamilton would be considered null and void under Danish law.

All of this is of little consequence anyway. James Hamilton left his family shortly after the move, never to return. And Rachel was left behind with two young sons and no recognized marriage.

Scholars also like to debate the year of Hamilton's birth. Some say he was born in 1755. However, Alexander Hamilton consistently said that he was born on January 11, 1757. The controversy comes from a probate document.

After Rachel's death, her first husband, Johann Lavien, claimed her estate for his son Peter. Lavien argued that the two Hamilton boys were not lawful offspring as was his son with Rachel. And a document was filed by the court to that end. In this "legal" document, the ages of the Hamilton boys is stated in such a way as to indicate that Alexander Hamilton was born in 1755.

This document was discovered more than a century after Hamilton's death. It offers proof to some scholars that Hamilton intentionally misled people about his age to appear younger when he arrived in the colonies. Most scholars who believe this presume Hamilton reduced his age to look more precocious. Yet it's also interesting to note that the aforementioned Danish court document also misspells Rachel's former last name. It spells Lavien, Lewine, thus weakening its apparently definitive claim.

In *Hamilton by the Slice* a different approach is offered. Alexander Hamilton is arguably one of the most brilliant men of his age. At least that's what Napoleon's Foreign Minister Talleyrand and a host of others thought. Therefore, it seems reasonable that Hamilton was born when he said he was. And it's equally sensible to conclude that Hamilton's parents were married, as he said they were, even if the marriage wasn't recognized on Danish Saint Croix.

The truth was a governing principle for Alexander Hamilton. In fact, Alexander Hamilton was truthful to the point of self-destruction. In the early 1790s Hamilton was led into an adulterous affair by a conniving husband-and-wife team who then blackmailed him. To stop accusations that the blackmail money was really involvement in illegal speculation at the Treasury Department, Hamilton wrote a public pamphlet that exposed his own personal foolishness. He preferred this rather than the allegation that he was a dishonest public servant.

Likewise, just before the Election of 1800, as Hamilton's Federalist party faced the party of his opponent, Thomas Jefferson, he again did the unthinkable. Hamilton criticized his own party's candidate, the President of the United States, Federalist John Adams, to key party leaders. In writing, Hamilton enumerated all of the reasons why he thought Adams was unfit to be reelected to the highest office. As Inspector General of the Army during part of the Adams' administration, Hamilton came to see the President as a man crippled by vanity and indecision.

Alexander Hamilton believed in speaking the truth, even when to do so was unpalatable or unpopular. Therefore, it seems highly unlikely that he shaved two years off the year of his birth in order to be viewed as a more gifted young man, or that he claimed his parents were married in order to soften his own illegitimacy. To put it as delicately as possible, if one doesn't believe Alexander Hamilton in the little things, it's quite likely that one cannot appreciate what he did and said in the larger arena.

Numerous Hamilton biographies exist, filled with details that one can quibble about, or not. *Hamilton by the Slice* has a different objective. It is written by one who portrays Alexander Hamilton in front of college and community audiences, routinely answering questions as the author believes Hamilton might have answered them himself.

This is not a critical study of Alexander Hamilton. Although it is backed by years of study, *Hamilton by the Slice* looks at topics of importance to Hamilton and to us. Each is a small stand-alone piece that aims at giving the reader a sense of what Alexander Hamilton, arguably America's most influential founding father, thought about particular ideas and topics.

Enjoy!

ACKNOWLEDGMENTS

Many people and organizations helped bring this book to life. As a first-person interpreter of Alexander Hamilton, I am grateful to all of the colleges, universities, libraries, businesses, organizations, and foundations that hire me. In fact, many of the topics covered in this book are those that audiences ask me about.

I am especially grateful to a few teachers who saw and encouraged my love of history. In public school, the two teachers named Mrs. Davis encouraged me "above and beyond." Professor Donald E. Emerson at the University of Washington, Professor Lowell Zuck at Eden Theological Seminary, and Professor Timothy L. Smith at The Johns Hopkins University offered freedom with structure. To all of them I am most grateful, although none of them, I suspect, would have predicted the wig and tights.

To the government of the U.S. Virgin Islands goes a particular word of thanks. An invitation to speak on the 200th anniversary of Hamilton's death at Christiansted, Saint Croix, in 2004, alongside historian Richard Brookhiser, Professor Stephen Knott, and Professor Joanne Freeman, marked the beginning of my fascination with Hamilton. I've been immersed in his writings ever since.

Regarding Saint Croix, I would be remiss not to thank Mr. and Mrs. Bill Cissel for the wonderful day we spent together on their native island.

Acknowledgments

Thanks are due to those who carry on Hamilton's legacy: Ron Gross, Professor James Pontuso, Professor Hal Bidlack, Lt. General Samuel V. Wilson (U.S. Army, Ret.), and Michael Pack and Sheila Hennessey of Manifold Productions. Likewise, I am especially grateful to Professor John Ferling, a gracious and generous student of John Adams and George Washington.

To Clay Jenkinson, Thomas Jefferson scholar and first-person interpreter, I am deeply indebted. For more than ten years, I sat across from Clay as host of the NPR program, "The Thomas Jefferson Hour." Clay's Jefferson made me want to know more about Hamilton.

Tony Macrini of WNIS, Norfolk, Virginia, also deserves special thanks. Tony routinely makes room for Alexander Hamilton and John Adams on his morning talk show. He is proof positive that talk radio can be intelligent and entertaining.

Many thanks to Billy and Mary Wilson for weekly affirmation, laughter, and true Christian fellowship.

This book would have been longer in the making if it hadn't been for some great advice received from Keith Cunningham, author of *Keys to the Vault*. He drilled it into my wife's head that "ordinary things consistently done produce extraordinary results." Along the same lines, James Malinchak deserves praise for helping to create urgency.

Hollis Guill Ryan found time in her busy schedule to edit the text. Sunny DiMartino designed and poured the book. Taunya Tae Waxham took Hamilton onto the world-wide web with our two sites: *www.HamiltonSpeaks.com* and *www.BillChrystal.com*.

Friend and housemate Steve Van Ness, descendant of William P. Van Ness, Aaron Burr's Second in the duel with Hamilton, keeps the farm running and us in stitches.

Janie Guill Chrystal made it all happen.

To God, from whom all blessings flow ... .

William G. Chrystal
Charlotte Court House, VA

Q & A
INTRODUCTION

Q **You wrote this book with a reader in mind. Who is your reader?**

A This book is for busy people who don't have the time to sit down and read an extensive biography. This is like a bathroom book—short glimpses of a great man, each one easy to digest in one sitting (no pun intended). It is made up of topics and Hamilton's thought about each one.

Each chapter begins with a quotation from Hamilton's writings or from someone who knew Hamilton. This is done intentionally so as you read them you will know I am staying true to the man!

Looking at Hamilton by topic makes it possible to get a clear sense of how he thought and what he thought. Many of Hamilton's views are timeless. They are unchanging principles that have implications for our own day.

Q **What is your ultimate goal with this book?**

A Alexander Hamilton is a great man. Too many times we think genetics or being born into the right family is what launches someone to greatness. Hamilton disproves these theories. He was born on an obscure island in the British West Indies. His father was a bum who deserted the family before Hamilton turned ten years old. Hamilton helped the family by becoming a clerk at a local merchant firm. Rachel, his mother, supported her two young sons with a small store, selling supplies, after her husband left but died of a fever within a year or two. Hamilton was barely eleven years old. He and his older brother then went to live with a cousin. Within a year, his guardian cousin committed suicide. This was definitely not a life of luxury!

So, how did Hamilton rise above these beginnings? He worked hard, kept the goal of "being more than a clerk" at the forefront of his mind, and befriended a minister who helped get him to the colonies to get an education. What all of this says is that Alexander Hamilton didn't have a leg up on anyone. In fact, he had to rise from lower depths than most of the other founding fathers.

My ultimate goal with this book is to show people it is possible to overcome challenges and not just survive, but thrive! Hamilton did just that and he did it by using only his God-given talents that he honed into razor-sharp tools.

Q What makes Alexander Hamilton a great man?

A I think his enormous self-taught and self-disciplined ability makes him great—his ability to think clearly; his ability to see what was really happening; his ability to absorb and master a topic; his ability to stay the course through heavy political fire; his ability to overcome obstacles and circumstances; his ability to understand human beings and their self-interest; his ability to put his own self-interests to work in the interests of the nation; his ability to be a behind-the-scenes influencer without needing to grab the spotlight; and, last but not least, his ability to envision and work for a future where the United States would be a "Hercules among nations."

Q How would you like readers to use this book?

A In my heart of hearts, I hope readers will use this book like a secular devotional. I hope they read the same topic a couple of days in a row and think about it periodically throughout the day.

I visualize the reader asking: "What are my own thoughts on this subject?" "How does this play in my life?" and "What can I gain by embracing and practicing Hamilton's view?" Or, maybe the reader will adopt a different approach by taking each subject and asking, "What is good or beneficial about Hamilton's thoughts on this subject?" Followed by, "What is negative about Hamilton's view on this subject?" Then the reader can wrap up the self-discussion with, "What is just plain interesting about Hamilton's thoughts on this subject?"

Q What were Alexander Hamilton's accomplishments?

A Hamilton had big accomplishments and small accomplishments. Which ones do I include and which ones do I leave out? I think it best to just give you a short list.

~ Overcame poverty without the help of parents and relatives.

~ Put his life in danger distracting a mob who came to tar and feather the President of the college he was attending, King's College.

~ Wrote a handful of widely distributed and influential political pamphlets.

~ Raised his own Company of Artillery for the colonies' war against Britain, the American Revolutionary War.

~ Earned the position of principle aide-de-camp to General George Washington during the Revolutionary War.

~ Asked himself, "What will this new nation need?" and spent his leisure time studying different forms of economies and governments.

Hamilton accomplished all this before the age of twenty-five!

His accomplishments from twenty-five on include:

~ Became a self-taught lawyer in New York.

~ Was an influential delegate at the Constitutional Convention.

~ Created and co-authored *The Federalist*, a series of 85 essays explaining the newly designed Constitution and prompting the masses to vote for the new governmental structure.

~ Was appointed the first Secretary of the Treasury in President Washington's cabinet.

~ Designed an economic infrastructure for the new nation that allowed it to be creditworthy and to gain in prosperity.

~ Founded the *New York Evening Post.*

~ Argued a case that eventually made truth an element in defining libel.

~ Allowed himself to be killed in a duel in which he never intended to fire. He did this on the off chance that he would survive and his reputation would be upheld. This way he could continue to be useful to his country.

Q **What can you tell us about dueling?**

A By the time Aaron Burr challenged Alexander Hamilton to a duel in 1804, dueling had been around for centuries. Men who fancied themselves as "gentlemen," particularly those with a military background, saw dueling as a way of resolving problems that the offending party didn't want to pursue through legal channels. Likewise, those matters for which the law offered no apparent remedy also occasioned duels. The sorts of things that brought on duels ranged from concerns over personal and family honor to disagreements about property ownership or who won a disputed game of chance.

Many well-known Americans fought duels. Andrew Jackson killed a man in a duel because of a horse race.

Commodore Stephen Decatur, who won fame during the War of 1812, was killed by another naval officer who accused Decatur of ruining his career. Alexander Hamilton's oldest son Philip died in a duel fought in 1801 with a man who said insulting things about the senior Hamilton. Henry Clay and John Randolph fought a duel because Randolph maligned Clay in the U.S. Senate (neither was wounded).

Duels did not always end in death. Sometimes, the parties involved reached accord by means of agents, or "seconds," enlisted on their behalf. Through correspondence and meetings between the seconds and the principal parties, satisfaction was sometimes obtained for the aggrieved party. When it was not, meeting in an out-of-the-way spot with swords or pistols (the favored American weapon was pistols) did not always prove fatal, either. Many duels ended after an inaccurate exchange of pistol fire.

When Alexander Hamilton met Aaron Burr, many rounds of correspondence had passed. But Burr was not mollified. He demanded the "interview" in Weehawken, New Jersey. "Interview" was the word used at the time to keep as many people as possible from knowing what was intended. Dueling was against the law. When someone killed his opponent, as Burr did, he faced murder charges. So did the seconds, who were charged with conspiracy.

After the duel with Hamilton, Aaron Burr was charged with murder in New York and New Jersey. Friends and family helped him flee to Georgia. A few months later he returned to Washington to preside over the Senate as Thomas Jefferson's Vice President. Jefferson's administration welcomed Burr with open arms. The New York murder charge was reduced by a grand jury shortly thereafter. The New Jersey murder charges remained on the books for three more years but there was no effort to extradite Burr to face charges.

Dueling was left over from a feudal age. Revulsion over the death of Alexander Hamilton did much to end public acceptance of it in the United States. It was Hamilton's last service for his adopted nation.

Q **If your reader has time to read only two chapters, which two do you recommend?**

A Beyond a shadow of a doubt, the two chapters would be Honor and Thinking. If you understand these two characteristics, you understand Hamilton!

Q **Any last thoughts?**

A A peer and close friend of Hamilton's, Gouverneur Morris, was one of our key founding fathers. He took the thoughts from the delegates at the Constitutional Convention and boiled them down into a readable, understandable document. We call this document the Constitution of the United States.

Morris delivered the eulogy at Hamilton's funeral. He asked the attendees to set Hamilton as the standard to strive for and always to ask,

"Would Hamilton have done this thing?"

It may be that without a vision men shall die. It is no less true that, without hard practical sense, they shall also die. Without Jefferson the new nation might have lost its soul. Without Hamilton it would assuredly have been killed in body.

—**James Truslow Adams,**
Hamiltonian Principles,
page xvi

At the time when our government was organised, we were without funds, though not without resources. To call them into action, and establish order in the finances, (George) Washington sought for splendid talents, for extensive information, and, above all, he sought for sterling, incorruptible integrity—All these he found in Hamilton. The system then adopted has been the subject of much animadversion. If it be not without a fault, let it be remembered that nothing human is perfect. Recollect the circumstances of the moment—recollect the conflict of opinion—and above all, remember that the minister of a republic must bend to the will of the people. The administration which Washington formed, was one of the most efficient, one of the best that any country was ever blest with. And the result was a rapid advance in power and prosperity, of which there is no example in any age or nation. The part which Hamilton bore is universally known.

... The care of a rising family, and the narrowness of his (Hamilton's) fortune, made it a duty to return to his profession for their support. But though he was compelled to abandon public life, never, no, never for a moment did he abandon the public service. He never lost sight of your interests. I declare to you, before the God in whose presence we are now so especially assembled, that in his most private and confidential conversations, the single objects of discussion and consideration were your freedom and happiness.

—Gouverneur Morris, eulogy at Hamilton's funeral by founding father and good friend

Hamilton was one of our first great nation-alists. "Think continentally," he counseled the young nation. He believed in the destiny of America and wished to confer upon the national government powers appropriate to its needs and opportunities.

—**Richard B. Morris,**
  editor of *Alexander*
  Hamilton and the
  Founding of the Nation

Chapter One

AMBITION

By some he (Hamilton) is considered as an ambitious man, and therefore a dangerous one. That he is ambitious I shall readily grant, but it is of that laudable kind which prompts a man to excel in whatever he takes in hand. He is enterprising, quick in his perceptions, and his judgment intuitively great.

**—George Washington,
letter to President John Adams,
September 25, 1798**

The year was 1798. President John Adams and the United States faced France in an undeclared war known as the Quasi-War. The French were instrumental in helping the colonies win the American Revolution against Great Britain. Now, a little more than a decade later, the United States declared neutrality and refused to help France in her war with Great Britain.

1

To add insult to injury, the United States negotiated the Jay Treaty with Great Britain and it contained economic and trading clauses. The French were furious and, in retaliation, they began seizing American merchant ships.

President Adams knew he needed both an Army and a Navy. He appointed George Washington to head the Army. Washington assumed the rank of Lieutenant General and he insisted that Alexander Hamilton be appointed the senior Major General to act as his second in command.

John Adams despised Hamilton and openly feared his level of ambition. Needless to say, he objected to Washington's request to make Hamilton second in command.

In the eighteenth century, people were raised on stories of Greek and Roman intrigue. Colonials feared ambitious people because ambition seemed to be one of the primary drives that fueled the passions of the ancients and led to so much mischief.

General Washington was right to distinguish between forms of ambition in his letter to Adams quoted above. In fact, Hamilton himself understood that ambition must be controlled. "Be virtuous amidst the seductions of ambition," Hamilton wrote his old friend the Marquis de Lafayette, in 1789, "and you can hardly in any event be unhappy."

Hamilton wrote these lines to Lafayette in a letter explaining that he would be the first Secretary of the Treasury of the new United States. He knew that much difficulty lay ahead. "I hazard much," Hamilton wrote, "but I thought it an occasion that called upon me to hazard."

Doing one's duty was more important to Alexander Hamilton than the reward and praise of his fellow citizens. In fact, doing one's duty was central to Hamilton's self-image.

His words to Lafayette regarding ambition have faint echoes to something he said in his first recorded letter, written in 1769 to his friend Edward Stevens. Hamilton was twelve years old and a clerk for an import/export business on the island of Saint Croix. "Ned, my ambition is prevalent, so that I contemn the groveling and condition of a clerk or the like, to which my fortune etc., condemns me and would willingly risk my life, though not my character, to exalt my station."

Alexander Hamilton would risk much because of his ambition. But he would not offer up his character, nor would he stand idly by while others did.

One of Hamilton's most devoted friends was the Baron Frederick William August Steuben, who began his military career in Prussia as an aide to Frederick the Great ... . This friendship began when Steuben landed in America in 1777, and joined the army at Valley Forge in 1778. Although he was Hamilton's senior by twenty-seven years, there was something very amusing about what might be called the reversal of relations, and the almost paternal interest of the young protégé in his middle-aged instructor, for it was the baron who first taught the American troops the orderly tactics of war ... but in spite of all his military genius he was helpless as a child in other things, and to Hamilton he looked for advice and help.

—**Allan McLane Hamilton,
grandson and author of
*The Intimate Life of
Alexander Hamilton***

Chapter Two

ARMY

─────── ⌣ ───────

The steady operations of war against a regular and disciplined army can only be successfully conducted by a force of the same kind. ... War, like most other things, is a science to be acquired and perfected by diligence, by perseverance, by time, and by practice.

—**Alexander Hamilton,**
***The Federalist*, No. 25**

In Hamilton's day, many Americans opposed a regular military establishment. History was replete with examples of governments toppled by their own standing armies. Plus, armies could be ruinously expensive. Besides, from its beginning, local militia (part-time citizen-soldiers) fought and won America's wars—especially those against Native Americans.

The French and Indian War (1754-1763), which was

a conflict between Britain and France over who would own the North American continent, began in the Ohio Valley. This war differed from previous American wars in that the British employed a large number of regulars in addition to local militia. This tactic helped them defeat the French and removed them as a threat to the colonies. The British employed the same tactic in the Revolutionary War or America's War of Independence (1775-1783); the overwhelming majority of British forces were regular soldiers.

Opposing them, especially in the first years of the war, were American forces that were overwhelmingly made up of militia units. Some battles were lost when poorly trained militiamen broke ranks and fled in the face of determined British attacks. And militiamen tended to be with the Army only for short periods of time before they returned to their homes. This meant that they could never be adequately trained.

There were no regular officers in the American Army at the beginning of the Revolutionary War. Some, like George Washington, had served with the British in the French and Indian War. There were also a few former British officers who had resigned their commissions and moved to America.

Later in the war, still other foreign volunteers arrived as well. Soldiers like Baron von Steuben, a former Prussian officer, helped to train the Continental Line, the regular American soldiers. Most American officers, however, were like Alexander Hamilton—eager amateurs who grew more experienced as the war progressed.

All of which is to say, the American Army was forced to depend on militiamen and amateur officers in most battles. Sometimes they fought valiantly, as Hamilton himself asserts. "The American Militia, in the course of the late war, have by their valour on numerous occasions, erected eternal monuments to their fame," he writes in *The Federalist,* No. 25. "But the bravest of them feel and know that the liberty of their country could not have been established by their efforts alone, however great and valuable they were."

As General Washington's aide-de-camp, Alexander Hamilton knew the larger truth. Without regular officers and soldiers, including the substantial regular force of its French ally, America's War of Independence could never have been won.

At a time when most Americans were thinking locally, Hamilton was looking at the bigger picture. Militiamen were fine for quelling local disturbances. But as Hamilton realized, even adopting a stance of neutrality required a standing army. And to repel foreign invaders, there was no doubt that a sizeable regular army and navy were absolutely necessary.

In the early days of his political life, Alexander Hamilton championed the need for a standing army. After a small one was established, he rallied for a larger force.

Hamilton was appointed Inspector General during the Quasi-War with France in 1798-99. This was an undeclared war with France who was interfering with the United States' merchant trading with Britain. Although the sea was the primary battle ground, Congress insisted that the United States prepare for a ground war. Hamilton worked incessantly to recruit and train a force but he didn't get much support from the President or, ultimately, from Congress. And one of the last letters George Washington wrote before his death on December 14, 1799, was to Hamilton discussing Hamilton's proposal for a Military Academy. Legislation to establish a Military Academy at West Point was signed in 1802.

Alexander Hamilton spent considerable effort convincing Congress and the people of the need for a standing army and navy. He firmly believed the newly formed United States needed a show of force to protect itself from foreign invasion. It seems likely that without Alexander Hamilton's efforts on behalf of an army and navy, the United States might not have been able to fight successfully the War of 1812.

Chapter Three

CHANGE

———— ∾ ————

The first step to reformation, as well in an administration as in an individual, is to be sensible of our faults. This begins to be our case, and there are several symptoms that please me at this juncture. But we are so accustomed to doing right by halves, and spoiling a good intention in the execution, that I always wait to see the end of our public arrangements before I venture to expect good or evil from them.

> **—Alexander Hamilton,**
> **letter to Marquis de Barbé-**
> **Marbois, February 7, 1781**

No longer in the Army, Hamilton wrote the secretary of the French legation in Philadelphia regarding a number of domestic issues. The passage quoted above expresses Hamilton's belief that the American government, in possession of a good plan aimed at

9

making it more effective, will succeed or not depending "on the choice of persons" involved in its execution.

The depth of Hamilton's psychological awareness is astounding. His observation that "The first step to reformation ... is to be sensible of our faults" sounds very modern. And his suggestion that institutions and people often do "right by halves" and spoil "a good intention in the execution" is a roadmap both for failed states and soured relationships.

The point here is clear: Alexander Hamilton knew how individuals and organizations think and operate. Like it or not (some didn't), he possessed a deep understanding of what motivates people for good or ill.

"Our prevailing passions are ambition and interest," Hamilton said during a debate at the Constitutional Convention in 1787 "and it will ever be the duty of a wise government to avail itself of those passions, in order to make them subservient to the public good; for these ever induce us to action."

Alexander Hamilton took the ancient Greek mandate "know thyself" seriously. In his view, human beings are ambitious and have many interests. (Hamilton uses the term "interests" in much the same way people today talk about "special interests.") Not only is this useful knowledge when designing a government, it's also helpful when looking at oneself with an eye toward change.

Being sensible—being aware—of one's faults is the first step toward reformation—toward change—for individuals and for nations. Yet such an awareness must also take stock of ambition and interest and how much they always play a part in our thoughts and actions.

Perhaps Hamilton's insight into ambition and interest was autobiographical. Many contemporaries considered Alexander Hamilton a dangerously ambitious man.

Or maybe this was the shrewd conclusion reached by someone who had spent a lifetime around powerful men. Whatever the case, such knowledge provided Hamilton with an astute vantage point from which to formulate policies and to respond to the actions of others.

Mr. Hamilton is one of the finest men in America, at least of those I have seen. He has breadth of mind, and even genuine clearness in his ideas, facility in their expression, information on all points, cheerfulness, excellence of character, and much amiability. I believe that even this eulogy is not adequate to his merit.

—Duke de Rochefoucauld-Liancourt, French Royalist and acquaintance of Hamilton

Chapter Four

CONFIDENCE

The manner in which a thing is done has more influence than is commonly imagined. Men are governed by opinion; this opinion is as much influenced by appearances as by realities. If a government appears to be confident of its own powers, it is the surest way to inspire the same confidence in others ...

**—Alexander Hamilton,
letter to James Duane,
September 3, 1780**

M any people were struck by Alexander Hamilton's self-confidence. Some interpreted his confidence as arrogance. Others were in awe of his mental gifts and boundless energy.

Hamilton himself, in the letter above, written to James Duane during the Revolutionary War, gives a clue to the source of his confidence. Not only did Hamilton have a firm grasp on his own mental and physical assets, he also understood the importance of how one projects oneself to others. As he stated in the letter, "if a Government appears to be confident ... it is the surest way to inspire the same confidence in others."

Hamilton was at the Battle of Monmouth fought on June 28, 1778, in New Jersey. He watched General Charles Lee lose his nerve in the face of a British attack. As a result, the troops under Lee's command became disorganized and retreated. General Washington stopped the men that day by placing himself in the midst of the routed soldiers and turning them around—involving great danger to himself.

Of all the lessons Hamilton learned on the field of battle, this may have been the most important. Individual leadership is often a matter of projecting confidence.

If a government or its leaders appear uncertain or fearful, the people will follow and the results are likely to be catastrophic. If, on the other hand, the government and its leaders offer calm confidence, the people will doubtless have the wherewithal to see things through to the end.

At an early age, Alexander Hamilton knew that a confident posture is an essential quality for a nation and its leaders.

Chapter Five

CRISIS

In such a state of things large and dispassionate views are indispensible. ... There ought to be much cool calculation united with much calm fortitude. The government ought to be all intellect while the people ought to be all feeling.
   —Alexander Hamilton,
   letter to William Loughton
   Smith, April 10, 1797

Alexander Hamilton was an astute student of human nature. He knew that people are more often motivated by their passions than by the "cool calculation" of their interests. And they are easily led by others. "Men are fond of going with the stream," he wrote James Wilson in 1789.

The on-going crisis with France in the 1790s gave Hamilton another opportunity to relearn both of these

15

lessons. France was angry with the United States for developing a relationship with their enemy Great Britain. To retaliate, the French disrupted U.S. trade by seizing American merchant ships. An American delegation was sent to France in the hope that growing tension between the two nations might be defused. But the delegation was refused access to Foreign Minister Talleyrand unless a bribe was paid to three of his agents.

When news of the French action reached the United States, many people felt that American honor was besmirched. War fever gripped the nation.

Of course, Alexander Hamilton wasn't surprised. He knew Talleyrand as a man with a great appetite for wealth. The Frenchman had spent many evenings with Hamilton when he sojourned in Philadelphia a few years earlier. Talleyrand had stayed in the United States in order to escape some of the more violent moments of the French Revolution.

Hamilton said to William Smith, "Our Country is not a military one. Our people are divided." Thus, although many Americans felt war was the only proper answer to French acts of treachery, war was precisely what the United States should not do.

Hamilton understood that the people's passions were justifiably inflamed. He worked hard to get Congress to increase the size of the standing army and to get new warships built. In fact, Hamilton was eventually appointed Inspector General of the new temporary army under his old commander, General Washington.

Hamilton used a characteristic approach: He urged allaying national fears by building up the military while calmly and carefully working behind the scenes to sidestep a military confrontation with France.

Hamilton's call to government, that it must be "all intellect," is a timeless insight. National leaders, especially in the midst of crisis, cannot afford to be "all feeling." They must cultivate "large and dispassionate views"; that is, they must see the big picture. To do otherwise threatens to become a fool's errand.

TO THE MEMORY OF

ALEXANDER HAMILTON

THE CORPORATION OF TRINITY HAVE ERECTED THIS MONUMENT

IN TESTIMONY OF THEIR RESPECT

FOR

THE PATRIOT OF INCORRUPTIBLE INTEGRITY

THE SOLDIER OF APPROVED VALOUR

THE STATESMEN OF CONSUMMATE WISDOM

WHOSE TALENTS AND VIRTUES WILL BE ADMIRED

BY

GRATEFUL POSTERITY

LONG AFTER THIS MARBLE SHALL HAVE MOULDERED TO

DUST

HE DIED JULY 12TH 1804, AGED 47

**—Epitaph on Hamilton's
tombstone**

Chapter Six

DEATH

~

My loss is indeed great. The brightest as well as the eldest hope of my family has been taken from me. ... But why should I repine? It was the will of heaven; and he is now out of the reach of the seductions and calamities of a world, full of folly, full of vice, full of danger. ... I firmly trust, also, that he has safely reached the haven of eternal repose and felicity.

> —**Alexander Hamilton,**
> **letter to Benjamin Rush,**
> **March 29, 1802**

Death stalked Alexander Hamilton all of his life. Not long after his father deserted the family, Hamilton's mother, Rachel, died of a fever. Hamilton was eleven. The cousin tasked with caring for Alexander and his older brother committed suicide within a year, leaving them virtually on their own. And near the end of the Revolutionary War, Hamilton lost his dearest friend, John Laurens, in a pointless skirmish.

The most difficult loss was the death of Hamilton's oldest son, Philip. He died in a duel on November 24, 1801. Dr. David Hosack was called to Philip's deathbed. Many years later he recalled that Hamilton, after looking at his son, took him by the hand and exclaimed "Doctor, I despair."

All who knew Hamilton noticed the difference in him following Philip's death. Among other things, he began to take more of an interest in religion. As he wrote John Dickinson, "Happy those who deduce from it (Philip's death) motives to seek in earnest a higher, and far more substantial bliss, than can ever be found in this chequered, this varying scene."

In April 1802, just a few months after Philip's death, Alexander Hamilton proposed forming "The Christian Constitutional Society." He suggested this in a letter to his friend, James Bayard, a congressman from Delaware. Hamilton believed this "club" would serve a couple of ends. The Society would support the Christian religion and the Constitution of the United States. But perhaps its greatest contribution would rest in its efforts to use "all lawful means ... to promote the election of fit men" to political offices.

This project resurrected earlier ideas Hamilton expressed about employing religion to strengthen the interests of the Federalist Party. It also was probably proposed with Philip in mind and with Hamilton's own growing interest in religion. Said Hamilton: "Nothing is more fallacious than to expect to produce any valuable or permanent results in political projects by relying merely on the reason of men. Men are rather reasoning than reasonable animals, for the most part governed by the impulse of passion."

In a move characteristic of the mature Hamilton, he would use the benefits of religion to defend the Constitution and assure that "fit men" were elected to public office. One cannot imagine a better tribute to his son nor a better way to channel his own grief.

He (Hamilton) evinced his gratitude for the attentions of my brother & myself by his attentions to us thro' life & by taking one of my sons to study law with him & refusing the least compensation.

—Hercules Mulligan,
with whom Hamilton
boarded in his early days
in New York

Chapter Seven

DEBT

~

It is a well-known fact, that, in countries in which the national debt is properly funded, and an object of established confidence, it answers most of the purposes of money.
> —Alexander Hamilton,
> "Report on Public Credit,"
> January 9, 1790

During the Revolutionary War, Alexander Hamilton copied quotations and paraphrases from books he was reading into his army pay book. Many of them came from an economics textbook by Malachy Postlehwayt, *The Universal Dictionary of Trade and Commerce*. He spent his free time understanding trade and commerce. He also studied the economies of the major European countries, especially that of Great Britain.

For Hamilton, Britain's economy was a model worth

23

imitating. He especially admired the British use of credit and debt, which as he noted in the opening quote, answer "most of the purposes of money."

When Alexander Hamilton became the nation's first Secretary of the Treasury in 1789, he inherited a terrible mess. There was no uniform national currency. Each colony produced its own. Furthermore, many of the Continental, state, and individual debts incurred during America's War of Independence had not been serviced or paid. And there was no national system of collecting revenue to collect funds to pay the outstanding debt.

The United States economy was a shambles and few foreign governments or banks were willing to loan money. And no national bank existed to fund national priorities.

Hamilton understood that credit and debt were essential for any national funding program. He knew the United States was weak and therefore, vulnerable to foreign invasion. As such, naval and military strength was essential to keep foreign nations at bay; and Hamilton knew these would be very expensive.

With an energy that defies description, Hamilton set to work. He established a system of revenue collection, standardized currency, and began paying interest on and/or paying off national, state, and individual debts.

At a time when most Americans engaged in agriculture, either on small farms or labor-intensive plantations, Hamilton saw that the future of the United States lay in a different direction. He envisioned a "mixed economy." And as Secretary of the Treasury, he attempted to move Congress to embrace commerce and manufacturing.

But Hamilton was no reckless advocate of runaway spending and deep debt. He knew that for a nation to have credit, its debts had to be promptly serviced and eventually paid off.

Alexander Hamilton always believed that a national debt could be a national blessing if the means to extinguish it was also present. Debt, like credit, could enable the young republic to do far more than it ever could do on a cash-and-carry basis. And, Alexander Hamilton did his part to ensure the United States paid its debt and created the trust relationship necessary to continue borrowing and growing in prosperity.

The General (Hamilton), in the practice of law, was literally a peacemaker. His invariable object seemed to be to discourage law suits, and to reconcile differences. And this character, united with his eminent qualifications for sifting right from wrong, in many cases, made him, a sole, and, in others, a joint arbitrator for determining controversies.

—**Robert Troup,**
Hamilton's longest friend
and colleague

Chapter Eight

THE DUEL

My religious and moral principles are strongly opposed to the practice of duelling, and it would even give me pain to be obliged to shed the blood of a fellow-creature in a private combat forbidden by the laws.

> —**Alexander Hamilton,**
> **Statement on Impending Duel**
> **with Aaron Burr,**
> **June 28-July 10, 1804**

O f all the chapters in Alexander Hamilton's life, the duel with Aaron Burr is among the most puzzling. On the surface, Hamilton had nothing to gain by facing Burr and much to lose, especially because he didn't intend to fire at Burr.

Alexander Hamilton and Aaron Burr probably first met in the army. After the war, they saw one another regularly, sometimes socially, and sometimes in court. Both were New York lawyers, and they appeared together as co-counsels on occasion and also opposed one another.

It was in politics that Hamilton and Burr were truly on opposite sides. Early on, Burr supported New York Governor Clinton's faction, which fought against a centralized government. Later, Burr worked to elect Thomas Jefferson and his fellow Republicans who also opposed a federal government.

Thus began a long rivalry. Again and again, in New York elections Hamilton worked to elect a Federalist slate of candidates while Burr sought office for Republicans.

The election of 1800 was arguably the most confusing in the history of the United States. When the ballots were counted, the one thing it established was that John Adams was not reelected. Thomas Jefferson, the presumptive President, tied with Aaron Burr, his presumptive Vice President.

In 1800, there was no Twelfth Amendment. This is the constitutional amendment that stipulates one candidate is running for President while the other is the Vice Presidential nominee. Therefore, according to the Constitution as it existed at the time, a tie for the Office of President had to be determined in the House of Representatives.

Complicating matters, the lame duck House of Representatives was in the hands of the Federalist Party. And a number of them thought Burr was preferable to

Jefferson even though it was known by all that Burr was really running for Vice President, not President.

Thus began a long political tussle. Thirty-six votes were taken in the House of Representatives, all ending in a tie between Jefferson and Burr for President. A thirty-seventh vote finally broke the logjam. Because of some strategic abstentions, Jefferson was able to take the White House while Burr became Vice President.

Alexander Hamilton played a role in Jefferson's victory. Although he consistently disagreed with Jefferson's views through the years, Hamilton thought he would be a more fit President. As he said to Gouverneur Morris, "If there be a man in the world I ought to hate, it is Jefferson. With Burr I have always been personally well. But the public good must be paramount to every private consideration."

For Hamilton, Aaron Burr was a frightening political figure. As he explained to John Rutledge, "'T is enough for us to know that Mr. Burr is one of the most unprincipled men in the United States." And Hamilton enclosed a confidential paper in his letter to Rutledge that detailed all of Burr's deficiencies.

Here are a few snippets: "His very friends do not insist upon his integrity." "In civil life, he has never projected nor aided in producing a single measure of important public utility." "No mortal can tell what his political principles are. He has talked all around the compass." "He is artful and intriguing to an inconceivable degree." And in a letter to James Bayard, Hamilton offered the *coup de gras*: "No man has trafficked more than he in

29

the floating passions of the multitude." In other words, Burr stirred up the masses for his own political gain.

One wonders why Alexander Hamilton opposed Burr so passionately, particularly since they'd always gotten along well at a personal level. The answer may be found in a Narrative written by Hamilton's friend Robert Troup in 1810. In it, Troup tells a story that Hamilton repeated to him—a story that Hamilton also shared with several other close friends.

Some scholars dismiss Troup's account, saying he was a gossip. But it best accounts for Hamilton's assertion, "With Burr I have always been personally well. But the public good must be paramount to every private consideration."

Troup's account reveals a frightening side of Aaron Burr. "What fixed the General in his opinion of Burr's designs was a conversation he had with him not many months before (the duel)," Troup begins. "In this conversation, Burr had the effrontery to accost the General in terms substantially like these. 'General, you are now at the head of an Army (This was when congress wanted to have a show of strength toward France and Hamilton was tasked with building a military force): You are a man of the first talents, and of vast influence. Our Constitution is a miserable paper machine. You have it in your power to demolish it, and to give us a proper one, and you owe it to your friends and the country to do it.' To which the General answered, 'Why Col. Burr, in the first place, the little army I command is totally inadequate to the object you mention. And in the second place, if the army were adequate, I am too much troubled with that thing called morality to make the attempt;' where-upon Burr replied in French; which translated is, 'poh! poh! General, all things are moral to great souls!'"

When Aaron Burr found out about Hamilton's role in the House of Representatives tie-breaking, he was undoubtedly livid. Later, when he heard of an account in which it was reported that Hamilton called him "despi-cable," he began the machinery that led up to the duel.

No amount of negotiation by designated Seconds Nathaniel Pendleton and William Van Ness assuaged Burr. He demanded satisfaction. On June 11, 1804, Hamilton faced Burr at Weehawken, New Jersey.

When Hamilton appeared that morning, he had already made it clear to his Second that he did not intend to fire. Therefore, why did he face Burr and the possibility of death?

The answer comes in Hamilton's own words. His presence at Weehawken involved "the ability to be in future useful, whether in resisting mischief or in effecting good, in those crises of our public affairs which seem likely to happen ..."

As odd as it seems, Hamilton needed to face Burr in order to preserve his reputation because without his reputation and his honor, he could no longer serve his country. In the final analysis, Alexander Hamilton faced Aaron Burr for the people of the United States of America. It was his final sacrifice for his country.

I distinctly recollect the scene at breakfast in the front room of the house in Broadway. My dear mother (Elizabeth Hamilton) seated, as was her wont, at the head of the table with a napkin in her lap, cutting slices of bread and spreading them with butter, while the younger boys, who, standing at her side, read in turn a chapter in the Bible or a portion of Goldsmith's 'Rome.' When the lessons were finished the father (Alexander Hamilton) and the elder children were called to breakfast, after which the boys were packed off to school.

—**James A. Hamilton,**
son of Alexander Hamilton

Chapter Nine

FAMILY
—❧—

*Experience more and more convinces me that true
happiness is only to be found in the bosom of one's
own family.*
> —**Alexander Hamilton,**
> **letter to Elizabeth Hamilton,**
> **October 25, 1801**

The letter from Alexander Hamilton to his wife
Elizabeth, quoted above, was written only a month
before their son Philip was killed in a duel. It expresses,
seemingly, a growing awareness in Hamilton of what
really mattered.

Political disappointments and the loss of access to
those occupying the highest offices in the land caused
Hamilton to rethink things. As he said to Gouverneur
Morris on February 27, 1802 (this was after Philip's
death), "What can I do better than withdraw from the

33

scene? Every day proves to me more and more, that this American world was not made for me."

One sympathizes with Hamilton. He had given his all for a particular vision of this nation. Frequent absences from his family, long hours spent writing government correspondence and drafting measures, poor pay in relation to what his talents would bring at the Bar, even the loss of his eldest son in a duel defending his father's honor; all of this and more was the price Hamilton paid for his adopted nation. After the election of 1800, Alexander Hamilton thought it was all in vain—all except for his family.

Hamilton did not grow up in a stable home. His father left Alexander and his mother and older brother when Alexander was about nine. A couple of years later his mother Rachel died; the cousin into whose care he and his brother had been placed committed suicide within a year.

Alexander Hamilton was a geographical orphan at the age of eleven. His father lived on a neighboring island but was unavailable to his two sons. As a result, his marriage into the large and loving Schuyler family in 1780, while he was still in the army, proved to be one of the best decisions Hamilton ever made.

Elizabeth Schuyler was a beautiful and intelligent young woman, the daughter of a well-connected landowner. She adored Hamilton—it was unconditional love—and Hamilton loved her and the Schuyler family just as deeply for the rest of his life.

Elizabeth was the perfect helpmate. Not only did she bear eight children and care for them attentively, including attending to their religious instruction, she also saw to it that her husband was always supported. As an old woman Elizabeth recalled helping Alexander write the draft report for the national bank. "I sat up all night, copied out his writing, and the next morning he carried it to President Washington and we had a bank," she remembered.

Like all relationships, theirs had its ups and downs. Elizabeth was forced to suffer through Alexander's puzzling affair with Maria Reynolds—an affair made public by her own husband Alexander Hamilton. The Reynolds' were a con team and they arranged for Maria to have an affair with Hamilton. After it began, James Reynolds, the husband, blackmailed Hamilton to keep the relationship quiet. James allowed the affair to continue provided Hamilton continued to pay. Later, James Reynolds was charged with being involved in an illegal speculation scheme. He decided to implicate Hamilton, and he told the authorities that Hamilton's blackmail payments were really payments into the scheme. Hamilton did not want the American people to think he had been a thief or speculator while overseeing matters at the Treasury Department. To squelch such rumors, Hamilton published and distributed a pamphlet outlining his foolishness in regards to Maria Reynolds and publicly apologizing for the affair.

There is no doubt that Elizabeth Hamilton should be credited with a share of her husband's brilliant successes. Without the foundation that she and the children provided, it is unlikely that Hamilton would have been able to work so hard, be pummeled so regularly, and then return, refreshed, to the political fray.

Elizabeth continued to support her husband long after his death. For the rest of her life (she outlived him by fifty years), she worried about Hamilton's reputation and did everything within her power to see that he received the honors in posterity that he had sacrificed so much to earn.

Chapter Ten

FOREIGN
ENTANGLEMENTS

───── ❧ ─────

*One of the weak sides of republics, among their
numerous advantages, is that they afford too easy
an inlet to foreign corruption.*
　　　　　　—**Alexander Hamilton,**
　　　　　　The Federalist, No. 22

Today, it's hard to imagine the political climate
that existed in the United States when George
Washington was President. The French Revolution was
viewed by some as an appropriate response to the American overthrow of British control. Thus, many Americans
sought better relationships with the new Republic in
France, including supporting it militarily. Others, Alexander Hamilton among them, realized that the United
States needed to develop stronger commercial relationships with Great Britain.

Yet Hamilton, better than most, also realized that the only hope the United States had for gaining in economic and military strength was to remain free of foreign entanglements. The United States would only be damaged by being drawn into Anglo-French intrigue. The reason for this is clear. By being a vassal of one or more of the European powers, the United States was no longer free to pursue its own interests but would be forced to support the interests of its ally.

French and British meddling in domestic affairs and their seizing of American ships, crews, and cargo on the high seas in the 1790s fueled popular passions. Many citizens picked sides. But Hamilton consistently advised President Washington to embrace neutrality as the only viable option for the infant nation. He had a number of reasons for doing so, not the least of which was that neutrality lessened the likelihood of foreign influence on American soil.

Nowhere is their collaborative spirit on this issue expressed more firmly than in the following passage from President Washington's Farewell Address, dated September 17, 1796. Long considered the work of Alexander Hamilton, the Address was inspired and outlined by Washington. Hamilton took his draft and expanded, changed, and polished it. This was a usual form of collaboration between the General and his former aide-de-camp.

"The great rule of conduct for us in regard to foreign nations, is, in extending our commercial relations, to have with them as little political connection as possible. ... It is our true policy to steer clear of permanent alliances with any portion of the foreign world... ."

Alexander Hamilton believed that the United States would one day be a powerful nation, a "Hercules." Until that day arrived, however, the U.S. needed to trade with Europe but not be caught up in its squabbles. Foreign influence and foreign war were unthinkable.

Today, the United States is indeed a Hercules among nations. And it's safe to say that Hamilton would view many things differently. One suspects, however, that he would continue to warn us against foreign entanglements. It is still not in the best interests of the United States to let any other nation have too great an influence over the American government or its citizens.

Hamilton's remarkable grasp of national interest was evident in the direction he gave to the foreign policy of the Washington administration. He was a realist. He saw nothing "absurd" or "impracticable" in a league or alliance of nations, but cautioned Americans against becoming "the instruments of European greatness." He believed that a power friendly today could become an enemy tomorrow, "that peace or war will not always be left to our option." ... Hamilton's guiding principles were prudence, realism, discretion in speech, moderation in action, concern for the national interest. "Real firmness is good for every thing," he once counseled. "Strut is good for nothing."

     —Richard B. Morris,
      editor of *Alexander*
      Hamilton and the
      Founding of the Nation

Chapter Eleven

FOREIGN POLICY

⁓

It is forgotten that mildness in the manner and firmness in the thing are most compatible with true dignity, and almost always go further than harshness and stateliness.
—Alexander Hamilton,
"The Defense, V,"
August 5, 1795

Theodore Roosevelt admired Alexander Hamilton. Nowhere does his indebtedness show more clearly than in the above quotation. "Speak softly and carry a big stick" is Roosevelt's fashioning of a Hamiltonian insight.

Hamilton knew that the United States would one day be a power on the scale of France and Britain. But that day was far off. Only by steering clear of European

41

wars could the infant republic organize its economic affairs and build its economy.

Then as now, many preferred war to diplomacy. This was no surprise to Hamilton, who realized that the people are "all feeling" when it comes to matters of national honor. The government, on the other hand, must always be "all intellect." And Alexander Hamilton helped to craft a thoughtful economic and foreign policy that was clearly in the best interests of the United States.

In the same essay as the one quoted above in support of the Jay Treaty with Great Britain, a treaty that aimed to resolve leftover problems from the American Revolution and to address ongoing trade issues, Hamilton wrote, "Nations ought to calculate as well as individuals, to compare evils, and to prefer the lesser to the greater; to act otherwise, is to act unreasonably; those who counsel it are impostors or madmen."

The survival of the infant American republic required peace. But as Hamilton assured the nation, it was not peace at any price. Serious questions of national honor and the preservation of permanent national interests, for example, could lead to war.

Hamilton clearly saw that the future of the United States would be better served by an economic alliance with Great Britain, not France. And such an alliance would undoubtedly at some point more greatly favor the powerful European nation, not the militarily weak United States.

Tolerating lesser evils while avoiding greater ones was necessary when dealing with European powers that were trying to use the United States as a bargaining chip in their own struggles with one another. The day would come when America could act from a position of greater strength. And when it did, Hamilton doubtless hoped the United States would embrace the maxim stated at the beginning of this chapter.

(Hamilton) was not an American, except by adoption, and could never have become president, though he was in some respects better fitted for the job than any other of the founding fathers. In a sense, he was the archetypal self-made man of American mythology ... .

—**Paul Johnson,**
author of *A History of*
the American People

Chapter Twelve

FREEDOM OF WILL (ACTION)

In the general course of human nature, a power over a man's subsistence amounts to a power over his will.
—**Alexander Hamilton,**
The Federalist, **No. 79**

When writing his offerings for *The Federalist*, Alexander Hamilton was especially concerned with the judiciary. Having "neither FORCE nor WILL, but merely judgment," as he put it, the judicial branch had to be kept as independent as possible from the other branches of government in order to do its job effectively. "We can never hope to see realized in practice, the complete separation of the judicial from the legislative power, in any system which leaves the former dependent for pecuniary resources on the occasional grants of the latter," he concluded.

Yet Hamilton's insight, stated above, was not only appropriate for raising up an independent, impartial judiciary. He later discovered this principle had deeply personal implications.

At the Constitutional Convention in 1787, Hamilton formed an informal alliance with a brilliant Virginian, James Madison. Six years older than Hamilton, Madison was known as a deep theoretical thinker and was one of the architects of the Constitution.

The two collaborated on *The Federalist*, a series of 85 newspaper articles designed to explain the embryo Constitution in such a way that it would be ratified in all the states. Hamilton wrote more than half of their number and Madison wrote the rest (John Jay wrote three installments but sickness prevented him from contributing more).

After their successful cooperation which helped bring about the ratification of the Constitution, Alexander Hamilton believed that he and Madison saw the task of government through the same lens. Imagine his surprise, after assuming the role of Secretary of the Treasury in President Washington's Cabinet, when Madison reversed course. As Hamilton wrote, "When I accepted the office (of Secretary of the Treasury) ... it was under full persuasion, that from similarity of thinking, conspiring with personal good-will, I should have the firm support of Mr. Madison, in the general course of my administration."

But almost immediately, James Madison, serving in the House of Representatives, did everything he could to block Hamilton's efforts. Said Hamilton: "Mr. Madison was actuated by personal and political animosity."

The explanation for James Madison's change in course is most often attributed to his collaboration with Thomas Jefferson, his fellow Virginian. Both seemed to see in Hamilton's efforts to create a national economic system a frightening lurch toward a central government that would not respect the power of the states.

While this may in part explain Madison's puzzling (to Hamilton) turnabout, the best reason may be found in the quotation which begins this chapter: "A power over a man's subsistence amounts to a power over his will."

After the Constitution was ratified, James Madison hoped to be elected as one of the two Virginia senators to the new government. But Patrick Henry blocked him. Henry "believed him (Madison) too friendly to a strong government and too hostile to the governments of the states." So said Spencer Roane, Patrick Henry's son-in-law. As Roane recalled, "In 1788, Mr. Henry nominated (Richard Henry) Lee and William Grayson as senators (taking the unusual liberty of nominating two) against Madison, and they were elected."

After antagonizing the powerful Patrick Henry by supporting the Constitution with its strong central government, James Madison was fortunate to be elected to the House of Representatives. Spencer Roane imagined that Henry's opposition did him good. " ... probably this rejection was useful to Madison, for, to regain the confidence of his native state, he brought forward the amendments (i.e., the Bill of Rights) introduced in 1789 in the Constitution."

James Madison was wealthy. Implying that there was a power over his "subsistence" is a figurative rather than a literal reference. But make no mistake about it, at home in Virginia, Madison had to reinvent himself in order to play a part in local politics and therefore, to have the opportunity to act on the national stage.

Madison and Hamilton were practically of one mind in Philadelphia during the Constitutional Convention. They worked hand in hand during the preparation of *The Federalist*. Yet once they returned from Philadelphia each had to take into account the views of the people back home.

Alexander Hamilton continued to labor against the forces in New York State who opposed the new Constitution. In Virginia, Madison joined with those very forces.

Their fruitful association came to an abrupt end. Hamilton, as Secretary of the Treasury, continued working toward a strong central government. While Madison, as a member of Congress, joined with those who favored more power for state governments.

It is impossible to know what course James Madison might have taken without the opposition of people back home. Would he have been a Federalist ally of Hamilton's? Or would he eventually have come to states' rights views on his own? Whatever the case, it seems likely in the early days of the new government that a power over Madison's political subsistence, really was a power over his political will.

Madison's defection initially surprised Hamilton. But

Hamilton's understanding of human nature and self-interest more than took it into account. If Hamilton had thought about it in advance, he could have predicted it!

Hamilton generally spoke with great earnestness and energy, and with considerable and sometimes vehement gesture. His language was clear, nervous (energetic) and classical. He went to the foundation and reason of every doctrine which he examined, and he brought to the debate a mind richly adorned with all the learning that was applicable.

—Chancellor James Kent, close and intimate friend of Hamilton

Chapter Thirteen

GENIUS

Men give me credit for some genius. All the genius I have lies in this, when I have a subject in hand, I study it profoundly. Day and night it is before me. I explore it in all its bearings. My mind becomes pervaded with it. Then the effort that I have made is what people are pleased to call the fruit of genius. It is the fruit of labor and thought.
—**Alexander Hamilton,**
conversation with a friend.
Found in J.C. Thomas, *Manual of Useful Information* (1893),
page 108.

There is no doubt that Alexander Hamilton was a man of genius. Thomas Jefferson said that he was "a Colossus unto himself." Chief Justice John Marshall said that standing alongside Hamilton was like "a candle next to the noonday sun."

51

But Hamilton, by his own admission, credited hard work and study for his success. French Foreign Minister Talleyrand, during a period of exile in the United States, marveled that when passing Hamilton's residence late at night, Hamilton was invariably hard at work.

Hamilton literally immersed himself in each and every subject. And sometimes the process struck others as odd or humorous.

Philip Schuyler, Hamilton's father-in-law, wrote Elizabeth Hamilton in 1789 to describe an incident that took place when Alexander was in the middle of mastering something. Hamilton "made several turns ... passing to and fro before the store of a Mr. Rogers," Schuyler explained. "Apparently in deep contemplation, and his lips moving as rapidly as if he was in conversation with some person—he entered the store, tendered a fifty-dollar bill to be exchanged. Rogers refused to change it," Schuyler continued, and "the gentleman (Hamilton) retired."

"A person in the store asked Rogers if the bill was counterfeited. He replied in the negative. Why then did you not oblige the Gentleman by exchanging It—because said Rodgers the poor Gentleman has lost his reason; but said the other, he appeared perfectly natural. That may be said Rodgers, he probably has his lucid intervals, but I have seen him walk before my door for half an hour, sometimes stopping, but always talking to himself, and if I had changed the money and he had lost It I might have received blame."

When approaching a subject, Hamilton did his best

to clear his mind of opinions and prejudices so that he could think about it in a fresh way. And when, as a lawyer, he needed to decide whether or not to accept a client, he often took a great deal of time before answering yea or nay. Hamilton had to think about all of the issues and implications that might be involved in the case before he agreed to represent someone.

In court, Alexander Hamilton routinely explored both sides of each argument. It wasn't enough to present his client's point of view. No, Hamilton needed to point out all sides of the matter so that the justice of his position would be clear.

The combination of hard work, immersion, and looking at issues from every possible vantage point contributed mightily to his remarkable success. For Hamilton, they were worth far more than genius.

Hamilton's fame indicates the unformulated but full appreciation of the unquestionable historic fact that he was the real maker of the government of the United States. Washington created, or at least caused to be created, the national entity; Hamilton did actually create the political entity.

—John T. Morse, Jr.,
Series Editor's Preface
in Henry Cabot Lodge,
Alexander Hamilton.
American Statesmen Series,
September, 1898

Chapter Fourteen

GOVERNMENT

The great question is: What provision shall we make for the happiness of our country?
—**Alexander Hamilton,
speech in the Constitutional
Convention on a "Plan of
Government"**

*Why has government been instituted at all?
Because the passions of men will not conform to the
dictates of reason and justice, without constraint.*
—**Alexander Hamilton,
The Federalist, No. 15**

When the Constitutional Convention convened in Philadelphia in the summer of 1787, most delegates realized that the Articles of Confederation were no longer able to bind the thirteen colonies together in prosperity. The Revolutionary War was won under its aegis. But any delegate with an open mind realized that great good fortune and the help of the French had more to do with victory than had the weak confederacy.

In addition, lingering problems left by the war complicated things beyond measure. The Continental Congress was unable to reach consensus on issues such as trade, debt elimination, mutual defense, and access to western lands. A new government was needed. And this would be called into being by a new Constitution.

The Philadelphia assembly aimed at nothing less than devising the means for a new government. And the views of the delegates varied widely as to how this could best be accomplished.

Underlying all the wrangling over concrete issues like how best to distribute the powers of government and how to achieve fair representation for all the colonies, there was a deeper issue. It had to do with the need for government in the first place.

To some, the confederation revealed plainly that a government without central power can accomplish nothing because its every act depends on the willingness of all the constituent parts to support it. Hamilton and Washington were among this number.

Other delegates, afraid of central power, believed that the representative component of government (House of Representatives) needed to be the strongest in order to protect the states from tyranny. These men worried about being swallowed up by a governmental leviathan.

Alexander Hamilton clearly understood that one branch of the government had to drive the others. He always favored a strong executive branch (President).

Hamilton was not especially afraid that the rights of the people would be violated by too strong an executive. He thought this was an easy matter to prevent with checks and balances among the branches of government. Far more worrisome for Hamilton was the fear that if too much power was placed in the hands of an unsteady body of representatives, with too many local ties, they would make decisions, popular at home, that did not serve the nation as a whole.

His position was grounded in history and in his knowledge of human nature. Government was necessary because "the passions of men will not conform to the dictates of reason and justice, without constraint." In other words, for Hamilton, government exists because the masses often cannot see and act in ways consonant with their own best interests or the interests of the whole. A government more focused on the needs of the nation and, ultimately, on those of all its citizens, is necessary to accomplish this.

Hamilton's view of human nature may have been darker than that of many of his peers. But such a view enabled him to see government differently from them. For Hamilton, government is necessary because the people cannot master themselves. Only government can be relied upon to provide the means to guarantee national survival and to insure the happiness of its citizens.

... it was Hamilton's institutions that gave us the greatness and the power that allowed Americans to pursue happiness.

—**Stephen F. Knott,**
author of *Alexander*
Hamilton & the
Persistence of Myth

Chapter Fifteen

HAPPINESS

—⌇—

It is a maxim of my life to enjoy the present good with the highest relish, and to soften the present evil by a hope of future good.
     —Alexander Hamilton,
     letter to Elizabeth Schuyler,
     July 6, 1780

Whenever Alexander Hamilton uses the word "maxim," the reader should take note. Frequently, Hamilton reveals what are, in essence, life principles by prefacing a thought with this word. And this letter to his beloved "Betsey," written during their engagement, is no exception.

What Hamilton expresses in this letter is what might be termed "learned optimism." And it is especially remarkable in light of his early years.

Never to return, Alexander Hamilton's father left the family when Hamilton was about nine years old. His mother died a few years later, after falling ill with a fever that nearly claimed Alexander as well. And to top it all off, neither Alexander nor his brother James received anything from their mother's estate. Her former husband showed up and claimed the small estate for his son, the Hamilton boys' half-brother.

James and Alexander were taken in by a cousin, who had a mulatto mistress and child. The cousin committed suicide shortly thereafter and, although the mistress and child were provided for in his will, the boys were, once again, left with nothing.

Both of the Hamilton boys had to fend for themselves. James became a carpenter's apprentice. Alexander, who was now eleven, continued working for the import/export firm that he had started with after his father deserted the family.

Alexander and James Hamilton were hammered by misfortune and greed. Saying that they had a rough childhood is a considerable understatement.

Yet Alexander Hamilton persevered. And, as he explained to his fiancée, he did it by relying on a life maxim: "to enjoy the present good with the highest relish, and to soften the present evil by the hope of a future good."

If it is true that one's "attitude determines one's altitude," it is no wonder that Hamilton succeeded so dramatically. Alexander Hamilton honed his mental faculties to a sharp edge and brought them to bear with unflagging energy. Even his political enemies praised his capacity for work.

Yet above all, Hamilton practiced cheerfulness and charity, doubtless with his life maxim in mind. Gouverneur Morris, an associate of many years, including serving with Hamilton at the Constitutional Convention, said at his funeral, "Oh, he was mild and gentle. In him there was no offence; no guile. His generous hand and heart were open to all."

When one compares the life that Hamilton lived with those of many of his political contemporaries—a number of whom enjoyed steady comfort if not actual affluence— one is struck by how far he traveled. Whatever the journey from Hamilton's birthplace on Nevis to New York represents in actual miles, it was an epic journey made victorious by Hamilton's tenacity, strength, and cheerful optimism.

Hamilton seldom despaired. The Federalist loss of power in 1800 and the death of his son Philip laid him low. But by hard work and a resilient good nature, Hamilton worked his way through even these.

Living, as we do, in an age of "victims," the example of Alexander Hamilton is compelling. One need not surrender to ill fortune, poverty, or the indifference of those nearby. As Hamilton reminds us, gratitude for present blessings and hope for the future are enough when combined with our own best energies.

His (Hamilton's) interest in educational institutions is well known, and in 1792, with others, he founded an Indian school at Oneida, and his name headed the list of trustees. This has since become Hamilton College. His public services were appreciated by many universities which have since become famous. As early as 1788 Columbia College ... made him a Doctor of Laws, while the same honor was conferred by Dartmouth in 1790. In 1791 the College of New Jersey, now Princeton, gave him this degree, and in 1792 both Harvard and Brown Universities followed the example of the other institutions.

—Allan McLane Hamilton,
grandson and author of
*The Intimate Life of
Alexander Hamilton*

Chapter Sixteen

HONOR

~

True honor is a rational thing. It is as distinguishable from Quixotism as true courage from the spirit of the bravo.

—Alexander Hamilton,
"The Defense, No. V,"
August 5, 1795

Anyone studying the life of Alexander Hamilton, sooner or later wonders what made him tick. Although he helped others amass great wealth, he wasn't particularly interested in money. And while he was the de facto head of a political party, he did not seek high office.

Even more baffling is why Hamilton, on several occasions, risked his personal reputation, his standing, and even his life, over matters that seem (to us, at least) relatively unimportant. Why did Alexander Hamilton

63

reveal in great detail to the general public that he was an adulterer and not a financial speculator? Why did he write a long treatise that exposed John Adams' unfitness for the Presidency even though a loss for Adams almost certainly promised the election to Hamilton's political opponent, Thomas Jefferson? Why did he agree to face Aaron Burr in a duel when Hamilton had no intention of firing back?

Hamilton's thoughts and actions are normally rational and brilliant. Can one assume, therefore, that the aforementioned episodes are a few self-destructive aberrations? Or, is it possible that they are also the deliberate acts of a consistent man?

Whatever the case, one cannot get at the heart of who Alexander Hamilton is without knowing what the word "honor" meant to gentlemen in eighteenth-century America. Especially among those with a military background, "honor" referred to a code of "dignity, integrity and pride" *(American Heritage Dictionary)*. Yet there is more; a reference from Hamilton's day in the 1771 *Encyclopedia Britannica* says that the word "honor" also involves "an exactness in performing whatever we have promised." Thus, for Alexander Hamilton not only does a gentleman value "dignity, integrity and pride." He must also do what he has promised to do.

In 1791, in a letter to his son Philip, Alexander Hamilton indicated how strongly he embraced this meaning of the word. Said the elder Hamilton, "... a promise must never broken and I never will make you one which I will not fill as far as I am able."

Nothing is more important than keeping one's word, Hamilton told his son. He felt as strongly about this as he did about speaking the truth. As far back as 1775, Alexander Hamilton embraced the motto, "Truth is powerful and will prevail."

Therefore, in order to show that he had not betrayed the public trust, Alexander Hamilton confessed to an affair with Maria Reynolds. It was better to confess an indiscretion than to be viewed as a dishonest public servant.

Likewise, when it came to the Adams pamphlet, Hamilton dismissed any notion that he wrote because of animosity toward President Adams. No, Hamilton penned his essay because "I should be deficient in candor, were I to conceal the conviction, that he does not possess the talents adapted to the *administration* of government."

Once again, truth is at stake—in this case the truth about John Adams. As a Federalist leader, Alexander Hamilton could not knowingly remain silent even if it meant a victory for the Republican Party. Hamilton, a man who always delivered the truth, no matter how unpalatable, could not sit idly by.

When it came to the duel, Alexander Hamilton listed all the reasons he should not face Aaron Burr: opposition to dueling on religious grounds, family, obligations to creditors, no ill will toward Burr, and, "lastly, I shall hazard much and can possibly gain nothing by the issue of the interview (duel)." On the other side of the balance sheet was only this: "all the considerations which constitute what men of the world denominate honor, impressed on me (as I thought) a peculiar necessity not to decline the call (i.e., Burr's challenge)."

The truth was Hamilton had impugned Burr's character. "He doubtless has heard of animadversions (i.e., critical or censorious remarks) of mine which bore very hard upon him," Hamilton admitted.

Alexander Hamilton hoped to serve his country in the future. If he refused to face Burr, his prospects down the road would be few. Attempts at mollifying Burr having failed, Hamilton did what his rational mind thought best. He went forward.

Honor demanded that Hamilton risk all; "everything to lose and nothing to gain." A gentleman had to be as good as his word.

Chapter Seventeen

KINDNESS

... a kindness consists as much in the manner as in the thing. The best things done hesitatingly, and with an ill grace, lose their effect, and produce disgust rather than satisfaction or gratitude.
—Alexander Hamilton,
letter to James Duane,
September 3, 1780

The above insight was cast in a letter to James Duane, a New York representative to the Continental Congress, discussing "the defects of our present system." In fact, Hamilton's point to Duane was that Congress' expenditures for the Army came "too late" and after too much debate to be viewed by the officers and soldiers with gratitude. After all, they were risking their lives for the country that was proving to be so stingy with supplies and equipment.

Even though he was talking about policy, it's apparent that Alexander Hamilton knew something about the subject of kindness. Is it possible that Hamilton's distinction between "the thing" and the manner in which it is proffered was a lesson from his difficult childhood?

When his mother Rachel died (their father had already deserted them), Hamilton and his brother James were denied a share of her estate by Rachel's ex-husband, who claimed it for his son, Peter Lavien, Alexander and James' half-brother. Placed with a cousin who committed suicide within a year, the boys were then parceled out again—James as an apprentice carpenter and Alexander as a clerk with the import-export firm of Beekman and Cruger (Alexander had started working there when he was about nine after his father deserted the family.)

In that period, Alexander was often the recipient of the "kindness of strangers." In fact, he owed his move to New York to a subscription fund raised on Saint Croix by the Reverend Hugh Knox, a Presbyterian minister who had taken an interest in the precocious young man.

We will never know for sure if Hamilton experienced both sorts of "kindness"—the one leaving a lasting impression and the other, a feeling of disgust. One thing is certain, however. In the last letter he wrote to his wife just before facing Aaron Burr in a duel, Hamilton begged Elizabeth to "be of service" to his cousin, Ann Mitchell. She "is the person in the world to whom as a friend I am under the greatest Obligations," he wrote.

The specifics of Mrs. Mitchell's kindness to young

Alexander many years before are unknown. But to say he felt grateful is an understatement.

"I have not hitherto done my duty to her," Hamilton explained to Elizabeth. "I have encouraged her to come to this country and intend, if it shall be in my power, to render the evening of her days comfortable. But if it shall please God to put this out of my power ... I entreat you to do it, and to treat her with the tenderness of a sister."

After Hamilton's death, Elizabeth received Ann Mitchell and took care of her like a sister for the rest of Ann's life. By honoring her husband's last request, Elizabeth was paying tribute to the sort of kindness that filled Alexander with lifelong gratitude.

In the practice of law he (Hamilton) was very conscientious in taking fees; making it an invariable rule not to engage in any case unless he thought it had right on its side. And he was accustomed to refuse larger fees than the nature of the suits and his services appeared to him properly to demand; being always desirous of receiving a fair and just compensation and no more. Where there was right, and no ability to prosecute or defend, he often rendered his services gratuitously.

—**Robert Troup,**
Hamilton's longest friend
and colleague

Chapter Eighteen

L A W

—— ∾ ——

Government is frequently and aptly classed under two descriptions—government of FORCE, and a government of LAWS; the first is the definition of despotism—the last, of liberty. But how can a government of laws exist when the laws are disrespected and disobeyed?
> —**Alexander Hamilton**
> **"Tully No. III," Dunlap and**
> **Claypool's** ***American Daily***
> ***Advertiser,*** **August 28, 1794**

A lexander Hamilton was a delegate to the Constitutional Convention in 1787. Afterward, he worked tirelessly for its ratification in his home state of New York. In fact, *The Federalist*, written in collaboration with James Madison and John Jay, were essays penned as newspaper articles to explain the Constitution in language that would assure its ratification in New York and other states.

But Hamilton knew that adopting and ratifying a new constitution would not ensure success for the republic. A key requirement for the government to be effective rests in the duty of citizens to obey its laws.

As he explained in George Washington's Farewell Address (Hamilton was his speechwriter), "This Government, the offspring of our own choice ... has a just claim to your confidence and your support. Respect for its authority, compliance with its laws ... are duties enjoined by the fundamental maxims of true Liberty."

During John Adams' presidency, in the midst of difficulties with France and Great Britain, Alien and Sedition Acts were passed by Congress and signed by the President. These changed the requirements for citizenship and allowed for the imprisonment of those committing slander and libel against governmental officials. In reaction, the State Legislatures of Virginia and Kentucky passed resolutions that said states need not comply with federal laws that are unconstitutional.

For Hamilton, this was a grave crisis that threatened to unravel the federal government. The duty of citizens and government is to obey the Constitution and law itself. If one dislikes particular statutes, there is a mechanism for getting rid of them.

"The basis of our political systems is the right of the people to make and to alter their Constitutions of Government," Hamilton explained in the Farewell Address. "But the Constitution which at any time exists, till changed by an explicit and authentic act of the whole people, is sacredly obligatory upon all."

Were he alive today, what would Alexander Hamilton say about civil disobedience? Would he understand disobeying a law in order to call attention to a greater wrong?

A more vexing concern would likely be the problem of selective obedience to law, occurring throughout American society today, but exemplified on the nation's roads and highways. Would Hamilton demand a greater effort to catch speeders, arguing that compliance with law offers safety for all? Or, would he conclude that there are too many laws on the books and that some of them need to be discarded?

Whatever the case, Alexander Hamilton would undoubtedly encourage American citizens to remember their duty to obey all laws until they are repealed or changed. After all, "the right of the people to establish Government presupposes the duty of every individual to obey the established Government."

It is given to but few men to impress themselves indelibly upon the history of a great nation. But Hamilton, as a man, achieved even more than this. His versatility was extraordinary. He was a great orator and lawyer, and he was also the ablest political and constitutional writer of his day, a good soldier, and possessed of a wonderful capacity for organization and practical administration. He was a master in every field that he entered, and however he may have erred in moments of passion, he never failed.

> **—Henry Cabot Lodge,**
> **U.S. Senator and author of**
> ***Alexander Hamilton,* 1898**

Chapter Nineteen

LEADERSHIP

*In popular governments 'tis useful that those who
propose measures should partake in whatever
dangers they may involve.*
    —Alexander Hamilton,
    letter to Angelica Church,
    October 23, 1794

Alexander Hamilton wrote the above in a letter to
his sister-in-law while accompanying the militia
to suppress the Whiskey Rebellion in western Pennsylvania. A group of small distillers refused to pay taxes on
their products and Hamilton convinced President Washington that their rebellion needed to be put down summarily. The laws of the government had to be obeyed,
Hamilton believed. Otherwise anarchy would prevail.

Hamilton was not only a careful student of human
affairs. He was a deliberate leader. It wasn't enough for

those in government to propose measures. They also needed to be at the head of affairs.

Yet for Hamilton, being at the head of affairs wasn't just a matter of marching at the head of a military force. No, good leaders also needed to anticipate appropriate future action.

During the Revolutionary War, Alexander Hamilton in his Army Pay Book wrote down a quotation from Demosthenes' *Orations* that he wanted to remember. It is a sentiment that, arguably, is at the heart of his understanding of leadership. "As a general marches at the head of his troops, so ought wise politicians, if I dare to use the expression, to march at the head of affairs; insomuch that they ought not to wait the event, to know what measures to take; but the measures which they have taken, ought to produce the event."

Good leaders don't wait for things to occur and then react to them. Good leaders make things happen. They are obliged first to calculate the best course and then, to put everything necessary into motion.

A careful study of Alexander Hamilton's life and work reveals how well he understood the importance of being proactive. Indeed, Hamilton often seems remarkably modern in his approach to leadership.

Chapter Twenty

MASTERMIND
GROUPS

——— ∾ ———

The ablest men may profit by advice.
> —**Letter from Alexander Hamilton,**
> **Concerning the Public Conduct**
> **and Character of John Adams,**
> **Esq. President of the United States**

The single sentence quoted above comes from one of Hamilton's most controversial essays. Hamilton wrote an unflattering essay about President John Adams' conduct in office. It was intended for a small number of Federalist leaders. However, it fell into the hands of one of Hamilton's political opponents, who printed it and circulated it well beyond Hamilton's intended audience.

It is unlikely that Alexander Hamilton's thoughts

77

about John Adams swayed any votes during the Presidential election of 1800. But it caused many in the Federalist ranks to question Hamilton's judgment and it earned him the enmity of John Adams for the rest of Adams' life.

In the essay, Hamilton raised a number of objections to Adams' personal style and to his administration of the Office of President. One important concern was Adams' unwillingness to consult with his cabinet. Said Hamilton, "Very different from the practice of Mr. Adams was that of the modest and sage (George) Washington. He consulted much, pondered much, resolved slowly, resolved surely."

Of all the proofs of John Adams' unfitness as President, none was more remarkable to Hamilton than not listening to his advisors. "A President is not bound to conform to the advice of his ministers (Cabinet)," Hamilton explained. "He is even under no positive injunction to ask or require it. But the Constitution presumes that he will consult them; and the genius of our government and the public good recommend this practice."

Alexander Hamilton believed that a wise leader listens to his inner circle. "Let it even be supposed that he is a man of talents superior to the collected talents of all his ministers ... he may, nevertheless, often assist his judgment by a comparison and collision of ideas."

Hamilton's mention of "a comparison and collision of ideas" sounds remarkably modern. One even thinks of the many "mastermind groups" that exist in business and industry today with just such an end in mind.

In fact, in his recollections of Alexander Hamilton, Robert Troup describes just such a group when Hamilton and Troup were students at King's College (Columbia University). "We formed ourselves into a weekly Club, for our improvement in composition—in debating—and in public speaking; and the Club was continued until we were separated by the revolution. In all the performances of the Club, the General (Hamilton) made extraordinary displays of richness of genius, and energy of mind."

Throughout his life, Alexander Hamilton believed in achieving the best possible results. Hard work and study can carry one far. But the best way to achieve extraordinary ends is in concert with others.

Assisting one's judgments "by a comparison and collision of ideas," gained by exploring issues with a wider circle, not only produces superior results. It is what good sense dictates.

While it is true that Hamilton had very decided opinions of his own, and undoubtedly was self-reliant and enthusiastically assertive, there is not a letter or published paper of his that indicates the existence of the least vanity or boastfulness—in fact, he never indulged in self-exploitation, but as a rule submerged himself.

—Allan McLane Hamilton, grandson and author of ***The Intimate Life of Alexander Hamilton***

Chapter Twenty-one

OPINION

———— ∼ ————

*Opinion, whether well- or ill-founded, is the
governing principle of human affairs.*
            **—Alexander Hamilton,
            letter to William Duer,
            June 18, 1778**

The letter, in which the above insight appears,
was written to William Duer in his capacity as a
New York Delegate to the Continental Congress. Among
other things, Hamilton writes about the quality of the
military force. He is particularly sensitive to the conse-
quences of having so many large, under-strength units.

Says Hamilton: "The goodness or force of an army
depends as much, perhaps more, on the composition of
the corps which form it, as on its collective number. The
composition is good or bad—not only to the quality of
the men, but in proportion to the completeness or incom-

81

pleteness of a corps in respect to numbers. A regiment, for instance, with a full complement of officers and fifty or sixty men, is not half so good as a company with the same number of men. A colonel will look upon such a command as unworthy (of) his ambition, and will neglect and despise it: a captain would pride himself in it, and take all the pains in his power to bring it to perfection. In one case we shall see a total relaxation of discipline and negligence of every thing that constitutes military excellence; in the other there will be attention, energy, and everything that can be wished. Opinion, whether well- or ill-founded, is the governing principle of human affairs."

If one were to summarize all of the above, it would look like this: Human beings see things through particular lenses. What is a blessing to a captain, bringing forth his best efforts, is a matter of indifference to a colonel, who feels himself underappreciated.

Human beings see things in a particular way, based on their own opinions and prejudices. And how one sees things determines what one gets.

If a colonel imagines that his command is insufficient, it will be. The leadership employed, or the lack thereof, will guarantee it. If, on the other hand, a captain sees his command as more than adequate, his energy and effort on its behalf will promote spectacular results.

For Hamilton, the immediate military problem was easily solved. Good organization—making sure military units were up to strength or were redesignated on the basis of their size—could remedy the problem.

But the larger concern remains. The mind is a remarkable tool. What it sees—or how it sees—often has more of an effect on what takes place than one might imagine.

Hamilton knew that human beings are filled with opinions and prejudices—many of which they aren't even aware that they possess. When people need to give a subject fresh thought, the only way it can be done successfully is this: They must work to identify and to isolate their own opinions and prejudices, and, having set them aside, proceed to look at the problem in a fresh light.

He (Hamilton) was ambitious only of glory, but he was deeply solicitous for you. For himself he feared nothing, but he feared that bad men might by false professions, acquire your confidence and abuse it to your ruin.

—Gouverneur Morris, eulogy at Hamilton's funeral by founding father and good friend

Chapter Twenty-two

THE PEOPLE

―――――― ∿ ――――――

It is an unquestionable truth, that the body of the people in every country desire sincerely its prosperity. But it is equally unquestionable that they do not possess the discernment and stability necessary for systematic government.
> —Alexander Hamilton,
> "Speech on the Senate of the
> United States," June 24, 1788

The voice of the people has been said to be the voice of God; and, however generally this maxim has been quoted and believed, it is not true in fact. The people are turbulent and changing; they seldom judge or determine right.
> —Alexander Hamilton,
> "Speech on a Plan of Government"
> in the Constitutional Convention,
> June 18, 1787

Alexander Hamilton has often been characterized as an enemy of the common man. To be sure, numerous scholars marshal comments like the second of those cited above to make their case. Some even employ a statement from Henry Adams, son of John Quincy Adams and grandson of John Adams, in his *History of the United States of America During the First Administration of Thomas Jefferson*. Adams seals Hamilton's fate as a people-hating elitist by repeating something that he supposedly said at a New York dinner. "Your people, sir—your people is a great beast" (Interestingly enough, Henry Adams gives no source for the "great beast" reference. Nor is such a comment found in any of the 26 volumes of Alexander Hamilton's papers.).

So, what did Alexander Hamilton really think about "the people?" Did he despise and fear them? Or did he know us better than we know ourselves?

Alexander Hamilton was himself a common man. He lived and worked among ordinary people all of his life. He experienced their strengths and their weaknesses, not out of books, but up close and personally.

Some of his political opponents who professed great confidence in the people and in their judgments did so from large, isolated slave-owning estates. Not Hamilton. As an eleven-year-old clerk on Saint Croix, as a company grade officer in the army, and as a practicing lawyer, Alexander Hamilton was given unlimited opportunities to see ordinary human beings as they are. And all of this experience taught him two things: (1) the motives of the people are usually good; and (2) they can easily be fooled.

Alexander Hamilton didn't despise the people. He took them as they are.

He knew the people so well Hamilton understood that, sometimes, it is the job of government to protect them from those who would lead them astray. Therefore, when something occurs to rouse the passions of the people, making them "all feeling," the government must counteract the situation by being "all intellect."

In *The Federalist,* No. 71, Hamilton says, "It is a just observation, that the people commonly *intend* the PUBLIC GOOD. This often applies to their very errors. But their good sense would despise the adulator who should pretend that they always *reason right* about the *means* of promoting it. They know from experience that they sometimes err; and the wonder is that they so seldom err as they do, beset as they continually are, by the wiles of parasites and sycophants, by the snares of the ambitious, the avaricious, the desperate, by the artifices of men who possess their confidence more than they deserve it, and of those who seek to possess rather than to deserve it."

For Alexander Hamilton, the greatest danger comes from "parasites and sycophants," from those who intentionally mislead the people in order to gain power and advance themselves and their own special interests. When such moments occur, the wise actions of the government are the people's best and only hope.

As he continues in *The Federalist,* No., 71, "When occasions present themselves, in which the interests of the people are at variance with their inclinations (i.e., when they are being misled), it is the duty of persons whom they have appointed to be the guardians of those interests, to withstand the temporary delusion, in order to give them time and opportunity for more cool and sedate reflection."

For Hamilton, the people aren't a beast. They are mostly good. But since they lack the "discernment and stability necessary for systematic government," the government must provide it for them. Alexander Hamilton sacrificed health, prosperity, family, and eventually his own life, to ensure a system of government that provided for all of the people, not just the rich and the well-born.

Chapter Twenty-three

PRAYER

Whilst at College, the General (Hamilton) was attentive to public worship; and in the habit of praying upon his knees both night and morning. I lived in the same Room with him for sometime; and I have often been powerfully affected, by the fervor and eloquence of his prayers.
—***Narrative of***
Colonel Robert Troup,
March 22, 1810

In the chapter on Religion, it is noted that Hamilton was not a churchgoer during most of his life. There were exceptions, as Robert Troup states in the narrative above, penned in 1810. Troup attended King's College (now Columbia University) with Hamilton and, according to Hamilton's grandson, Allan McLane Hamilton, "There was probably no more attached friend than Troup."

While at King's College, Hamilton was still very interested in religion. This was an outgrowth of his relationship with the Presbyterian minister, the Reverend Hugh Knox, on the island of Saint Croix where Hamilton spent his childhood. According to Troup, "The General (Hamilton) had read most of the polemical writers on Religious subjects; and he was a zealous believer in the fundamental doctrines of Christianity; and I confess that the arguments with which he was accustomed to justify his belief, have tended, in no small degree, to confirm my own faith in revealed Religion."

Troup was especially taken with Hamilton's prayers, uttered on his knees openly, morning and night, in the presence of his roommates. And Troup maintains that Hamilton continued this custom after he joined the army. "When he commanded a company of Artillery in the summer of 1776, I paid him a visit; and at night, and in the morning, he went to prayer in his usual mode."

Alexander Hamilton was no deist, like other founding fathers such as Thomas Jefferson and Benjamin Franklin. Hamilton's God was not a clockmaker who started the world in motion and then retreated from it. Hamilton believed in a God who is active in the lives of people. And while he did not attend church after his college years, Hamilton never hesitated to help the poor or to encourage his wife Elizabeth in her own exercise of faith.

Furthermore, Hamilton seems to have remained a man of prayer. His son James remembered as a twelve-year-old spending the Tuesday night before the duel, which took place on Wednesday, with his father. Especially memorable was how he and Hamilton recited the Lord's Prayer in unison.

After being mortally wounded by Aaron Burr, Hamilton was taken from Weehawken, New Jersey, back to New York City, where he lay near death in the home of William Bayard. Shortly after being taken there, Hamilton directed that a message be sent to Benjamin Moore, the Episcopal Bishop of New York, asking for Holy Communion.

After arriving at the Bayard home, he "proceeded to converse with him on the subject of his receiving the Communion," Bishop Moore later recalled. "Do you sincerely repent of your sins past? Have you a lively faith in God's mercy through Christ? ... And are you disposed to live in love and charity with all men?"

Recalled the Bishop, "He lifted up his hands and said: 'With the utmost sincerity of heart I can answer those questions in the affirmative. I have no ill-will against Colonel Burr. I met him with a fixed resolution to do him no harm. I forgive all that happened.'" Bishop Moore then offered the sacrament "which he received with great devotion, and his heart afterwards appeared to be perfectly at rest."

Alexander Hamilton didn't attend church services for the majority of his life. Hence, scholars tend to view his faith with suspicion. Yet faith for most people is largely a private matter. And it shouldn't surprise anyone that Hamilton didn't say much about it.

It is clear that Alexander Hamilton, at least at certain times in his life, was zealous in prayer. Likewise, at the very end of his life, he sought the comforts of the Christian faith, namely Holy Communion and prayer. And these, clearly, brought him great comfort and peace in his final hours.

Chapter Twenty-four

RELIGION

To all those dispositions which promote political happiness, Religion and Morality are essential props.
—**Draft of George Washington's**
***Farewell Address* written by**
Alexander Hamilton, July 30, 1796

As a political thinker, Alexander Hamilton appreciated the importance of religion. Like nothing else, religion helps to inculcate civic virtue. Religious people tend to be respectful and law-abiding.

In addition, Hamilton reasoned that the United States has something to offer that is "far more precious than mere religious toleration." In the "Report on Manufactures," he explains that in America, one finds "a perfect equality of religious privileges." And this will eventually attract European immigrants eager to "pursue their own trades and professions."

Although a number of the founding fathers understood the civic benefit of religious freedom, Alexander Hamilton was undoubtedly the first of them to see its economic side. His was a prophetic insight. How many European immigrants who reached America's shores in the late nineteenth and early twentieth centuries did so because of religious freedom?

When John Adams lost the presidential election in 1800, Hamilton also thought that religion could be of service to the Federalist Party. Writing James Bayard, a Delaware congressman, he proposed "The Christian Constitutional Society." It would support the Christian religion and the Constitution of the United States, and it would work to elect "fit men" to office.

It is possible that one reason Alexander Hamilton saw the benefits of religion to society so clearly is because he was a Christian. Hugh Knox, a Presbyterian minister on Saint Croix where Hamilton spent his boyhood, had a pronounced influence on the young Hamilton. Not only did he organize the subscription fund that enabled Hamilton to go to the colonies and to get an education, Knox also took him under his religious wing.

Nowhere is Knox's influence on Hamilton's religious life more apparent than in a letter Hamilton wrote (he was 15) describing the destruction that a hurricane caused when it hit the island. More sermon than narrative, it could have been written by a Presbyterian minister. "Look back Oh! my soul, look back and tremble," Hamilton writes. "Rejoice at thy deliverance, and humble thyself in the presence of thy deliverer."

94

With survivor's guilt in the back of his mind, Hamilton goes on; "Yet hold, Oh vain mortal! Check thy ill timed joy. Art thou so selfish to exult because thy lot is happy in a season of universal woe? Hast thou no feelings for the miseries of thy fellow creatures?"

Alexander Hamilton was not a churchgoer, except for a period during college. Writing his friend John Laurens during the Revolutionary War on "the subject of wife," Hamilton said, "As to religion a moderate stock will satisfy me. She must believe in God and hate a saint."

He was probably describing himself at the time. After the death of his son Philip in 1801, however, Hamilton seems to have turned once again to religion. And by the time he faced his own death in a duel with Aaron Burr in 1804, it's clear that he had returned to the faith of his childhood.

In his last letter to his wife Elizabeth, written the night before his duel with Aaron Burr, Alexander Hamilton explains that he won't fire at Burr. "The scruples of a Christian have determined me to expose my own life to any extent, rather than subject myself to the guilt of taking the life of another. This much increase my hazards, and redoubles my pangs for you," he wrote.

After being mortally wounded in the duel on July 11, 1804, Alexander Hamilton forgave Aaron Burr. He also requested and received Holy Communion.

Alexander Hamilton died a Christian.

Sir Walter Hely-Hutchinson, late Governor of Cape Colony (South Africa), wrote to Hamilton's grandson, Allan McLane Hamilton, who is the author of *The Intimate Life of Alexander Hamilton* in January, 1910:

... The unificationists went about, so to speak, with a copy of Alexander Hamilton's 'Life' in one pocket, and a copy of the Federalist in the other, preaching unification, and advising their friends to read, before making up their minds against unification, about the birth-throes of the Constitution of the United States; and to note Hamilton's words of wisdom both as to the weakness likely to arise from over-assertion of State rights, and as to the folly of rejecting a Constitution which was, of necessity, a compromise, merely because some of its provisions did not square with one's own particular or particularist views.

—Allan McLane Hamilton,
grandson and author of
The Intimate Life of
Alexander Hamilton

Chapter Twenty-five

SLAVERY

The only distinction between freedom and slavery consists in this: In the former state a man is governed by the laws to which he has given his consent, either in person, or by his representatives; in the latter, he is governed by the will of another. In the one case, his life and property are his own; in the other, they depend upon the pleasure of his master.
—**Alexander Hamilton,**
A Full Vindication of
the Measures of Congress,
December 15, 1774

When the Declaration of Independence was adopted by the Second Continental Congress on July 4, 1776, nearly half of those voting for it owned slaves. Clearly, the Declaration's lofty rhetoric, "we hold these truths to be self evident that all men are created equal," did not really apply to all men. This prompted

97

one English observer to comment that those who yelped most about liberty also had whips in one hand to beat frightened slaves.

Of all those who rallied to the cause of liberty at that time, Alexander Hamilton was in a rather unique position when it came to slavery. Although he did not own slaves, he knew as much about the "peculiar institution," as it was called by some, as did any slave owner or trader. Hamilton's employer on the island of Saint Croix, Nicholas Cruger, regularly received shipments of slaves from Africa and sold them at the market. When the ill Cruger went to New York to recuperate, he left fourteen-year-old Hamilton to conduct all of his business.

One of the most poignant letters Hamilton wrote during the period when he was left in charge by Nicholas Cruger describes the arrival of a ship carrying slaves, or "mules" as they were called. "A worse parcel" of them, Hamilton wrote his employer Nicholas Cruger, "was never seen." In a matter of fact tone, the young clerk explains that of 48 slaves embarked on the ship, seven died in transit. And he had already taken measures to put the others out to "pasture" to regain their health.

It is clear that Alexander Hamilton was doing his best to nurse the ill slaves back to health. His job was to get the best possible price for them and he was angling to do just that.

A fourteen or fifteen-year-old clerk on the Island of Saint Croix, probably didn't have many options when it came to making a living. Hamilton may not have wanted anything to do with slavery. But the truth of the matter is

98

that Alexander Hamilton was involved in the slave trade.

What did Hamilton think about slavery? The essay quoted above, written at the beginning of the American Revolution to explain why the colonists must separate from Great Britain, makes it clear that Hamilton was under no illusions about slavery. A slave "is governed by the will of another," he writes.

But unlike many founding fathers, Alexander Hamilton did not make an easy peace with slavery. During the Revolutionary War, Hamilton and his friend John Laurens proposed raising "three or four battalions of negroes." Explaining the plan to John Jay, Hamilton notes, "The contempt we have been taught to entertain for the blacks, makes us fancy many things that are founded neither in reason nor experience."

Their "natural faculties are probably as good as ours," Hamilton reckoned. They will make excellent soldiers and, if anything, because of the "habit of subordination" they are obliged to "acquire from a life of servitude," they will require less time to train than their white counterparts.

Not surprisingly, the plan to raise African-American battalions went nowhere. But soon after the war, in 1785, Alexander Hamilton became a founding member of the New York Society for Promoting the Manumission of Slaves and a member of a steering committee "to Report a Line of Conduct to be recommended."

The line of conduct taken was this: On March 13, 1786, Hamilton was one of those who signed a petition to the New York Legislature urging the end of the slave trade. It was, the petition said, a horrid commerce, "repugnant to humanity." A free and enlightened people must never sanction something so "inconsistent with liberality and justice."

Like many Americans, Alexander Hamilton was implicated in the institution of slavery. Unlike most of them, he publicly spoke against it.

Chapter Twenty-six

STATES' RIGHTS

There are certain social principles in human nature, from which we may draw the most solid conclusions with respect to the conduct of individuals and of communities. We love our families more than our neighbors; we love our neighbors more than our countrymen in general. The human affections, like the solar heat, lose their intensity as they depart from the centre; and become languid in proportion to the expansion of the circle on which they act.

—Alexander Hamilton,
speech at the New York
Ratifying Convention on the
Distribution of Powers,
June 27, 1788

It is difficult today to realize how much acrimony accompanied politics in the first years of the United States. Many people genuinely feared totalitarian rule.

And to some of those people, the new Constitution granted way too much power to the executive branch of government.

Alexander Hamilton's activities as Secretary of the Treasury did little to allay their fears. By arguing for the assumption of all state, national, and individual debts, creating a national bank, and proposing a standing army and a navy with the taxes necessary to support them, Hamilton seemed to be the exemplar for the large central government they feared. Hamilton's political opponents, in particular, operating under the banner of states' rights, were convinced that Hamilton was doing everything he could to fashion a government that would swallow up individual states.

Alexander Hamilton understood the argument for states' rights more deeply than most of his opponents might guess. "The attachment of the individual will be first and for ever secured by the State governments," Hamilton had told the New York Ratifying Convention. "Wherever the popular attachments be, there will rest the political superiority."

Furthermore, in *The Federalist,* No. 27, he explored the difficulty for a distant government to influence its citizens. "Man is very much a creature of habit. A thing that rarely strikes his senses will generally have but little influence upon his mind. A government continually at a distance and out of sight can hardly be expected to interest the sensations of the people." Because state governments are closer to the people than the federal government, for Hamilton, it went without saying that they would command more loyalty from their constituents.

Hamilton hoped to make the federal government more a part of people's lives (commanding more of their loyalty). Nonetheless he genuinely understood the attachment of people to the states in which they lived.

Because he was born outside the United States, it has been suggested that Alexander Hamilton had no particular loyalty to any state, including New York where he lived most of his American life. Some have even said that his outlook was more "American" because of his foreign birth.

While that may be, Alexander Hamilton absorbed both the idea that human affections are stronger the closer one is to home and the argument that by vesting most of the power of government in individual states, the danger of strong government ("monarchy" as it was so often caricatured) would be averted.

Hamilton knew both points of view. But he never failed to support a strong federal government with an energetic executive. For him, it was the only government able to undertake the work necessary to make the United States a great nation.

It is almost superfluous to say that Hamilton's greatest literary work was done in writing the major part of The Federalist, ... acknowledged to be the ablest treatise on our Constitution which has ever been or is likely to be written ... . Hamilton's contributions were made at a trying time, when he was giving himself body and soul to the formation for, and adoption of, a Constitution by discontented patriots. Incidentally he went hither and thither to try his cases. These productions (The Federalist) were composed under the most uncomfortable circumstances—in the cabin of a small Hudson River sloop; by the light of a dim candle in a country inn; in fact, they were regarded by their author only as essays for suggestive and contemporary use.

—Allan McLane Hamilton,
grandson and author of
The Intimate Life of
Alexander Hamilton

Chapter Twenty-seven

THINKING

_The best way of determining disputes and of inves-
tigating truth, is by descending to elementary
principles. Any other method may only bewilder
and misguide the understanding._
—Alexander Hamilton,
The Farmer Refuted,
February 23, 1775

Alexander Hamilton was a sophisticated, creative
thinker who employed two techniques in order
to achieve clear thought. In _The Federalist,_ No. 31,
Hamilton explains his methodology.

"In disquisitions of every kind, there are certain primary truths, or first principles, upon which all subse-
quent reasonings must depend," he writes. "These
contain an internal evidence which, antecedent to all
reflection or combination, commands the assent of the

mind. Where it produces not this effect, it must proceed either from some defect or disorder in the organs of perception, or from the influence of some strong interest, or passion, or prejudice."

Primary truths or elementary principles automatically command the mind, Hamilton asserts. And when they don't, it's safe to assume they are blocked by one's lack of clear perception or because of "the influence of some strong interest, or passion, or prejudice." Thus, the first technique employed by Hamilton when looking at an issue or problem is to use a time-honored maxim as a guide.

There are "maxims in geometry," Hamilton explains in *The Federalist,* No. 31: "The whole is greater than its part; things equal to the same are equal to one another; two straight lines cannot enclose a space; and all right angles are equal to each other."

Just as clearly, there are "maxims in ethics and politics," he writes. "There cannot be an effect without a cause" is one of them. "... the means ought to be proportioned to the end ... every power ought to be commensurate with its object ... there ought to be no limitation of a power destined to effect a purpose which itself is incapable of limitation," and so on.

For Alexander Hamilton, these "maxims in ethics and politics" are almost as sure a guide to clear reasoning as are their mathematical counterparts. Yet where these maxims fail to yield clear thinking, Hamilton was sure there was another explanation. He knew that "interest, or passion, or prejudice" had intervened.

Ever wary of the mind's ability to lead people astray, Hamilton knew that human beings must use intellectual guides and they must also thoroughly scour their own viewpoints in order to put aside interests, passions, and prejudices.

"Men, upon too many occasions, do not give their own understandings fair play; but, yielding to some untoward bias, they entangle themselves in words and confound themselves in subtleties," Hamilton writes in *The Federalist,* No. 31. Only by clearing away their biases and by careful reasoning using time-honored maxims, could human beings do their best thinking.

James A. Hamilton, the son of Alexander Hamilton, discovered a copy of George Washington's Farewell Address, written in his father's handwriting—suggesting that his father wrote it. James then wrote to a friend of his father. He asked the friend to comment on it.

George Cabot wrote to James: *"When that address was published, it was understood among your father's friends that it was written by him. It was, however, considered important that it should have the influence of Washington's name and character, and I must advise that until it has ceased to do its work, the question of the authorship should not be discussed."*

—**Allan McLane Hamilton,**
grandson and author of
The Intimate Life of
Alexander Hamilton

Chapter Twenty-eight

TRUTH & OPENNESS

'T is my maxim to let the plain, naked truth speak for itself: and if men won't listen to it, 't is their own fault: they must be contented to suffer for it.
—**Alexander Hamilton,**
A Vindication of the Full
Measures of the Congress,
December 15, 1774

Alexander Hamilton valued truth and openness as did few others of his age. Gouverneur Morris, at Hamilton's funeral, recalled that at the Constitutional Convention in Philadelphia, Hamilton signed the compact while expressing "his apprehension that it did not contain sufficient means of strength for its own preservation; and that in consequence we should share the fate of many other republics and pass through Anarchy to Despotism."

"On this important subject he never concealed his opinion," Morris exclaimed. "He disdained concealment."

In these remarks of Gouverneur Morris, one finds a key to understanding what made Alexander Hamilton tick. Hamilton believed in speaking the truth and in letting the chips fall where they may.

His political and personal style was in sharp contrast to those of many of his contemporaries. Indirection was popular in Hamilton's day. This involves getting other people to do one's bidding and to sign their name to the act. Thus, when the issue in question becomes public, the instigator is able to claim innocence, making it seem as if the deed was the work of others and not his own.

Hamilton disliked such strategies. To him, they lacked character.

There is no better example of indirection than the Kentucky and Virginia Resolutions. Secretly written by Thomas Jefferson, Vice President of the United States, and James Madison, a Member of Congress, these documents were presented to the state legislatures of the aforementioned states and passed into law. In a nutshell, the Kentucky and Virginia Resolutions said that the respective states need not obey the Alien and Sedition Acts because they were unconstitutional. The laws at which the Resolutions were aimed lengthened the time required for citizenship and allowed seditious journalists to be thrown into jail.

For Hamilton, laws must be obeyed or repealed. And barring that, the courts stand ready to determine whether the laws in question are constitutional or not.

Jefferson and Madison, both of them under oath to "uphold and defend the Constitution of the United States," under a cloak of secrecy, took an improper course to reach their goal. They defied the Constitution and threatened the Union. Yet each was able to deny any involvement.

For Hamilton, if they didn't like the laws in question, the Virginia gentlemen, like anyone else, could work for their repeal or for the passage of new laws. But the route they chose, working secretly, defied the power of the federal government and its right to make laws. (After Jefferson became President of the United States, the Alien and Sedition Acts, previously passed by Congress and signed into law by President John Adams, expired.)

Hamilton hated concealment. He believed in speaking the truth and in openly clashing with his opponents. And when he wrote for the press, using pseudonyms as did all writers of his day, he made no attempt to alter his style so that people might think someone else was writing.

In 1795, in a letter to Oliver Wolcott, who succeeded him at the Treasury Department, Hamilton wrote about a mutual acquaintance, "To do mischief he must work in the Dark."

This is why Hamilton prized openness and hated indirection. The only reason for working in the dark is to cause mischief. And mischief, in government, only

111

serves to weaken the Federal Union and hence, to undermine the Republic.

Alexander Hamilton disdained those who operated under the cover of darkness. He much preferred working out in the open.

Chapter Twenty-nine

WAR

Wars oftener proceed from angry and perverse passions than from cool calculation of interest.
—**Alexander Hamilton,**
letter to George Washington,
April 14, 1794

It is worth noting that the quotation above from Alexander Hamilton appears in a letter to George Washington that begins with the observation, "It is the duty of every man ... to contribute all in his power towards preventing evil and producing good." For Hamilton, during the 1790s, this meant avoiding war at all costs.

On February 6, 1778, during the Revolutionary War, representatives of the Continental Congress signed a treaty with Louis XVI that pledged mutual support in wartime. Fifteen years later, France called in its marker. Though the French Revolution had occurred and Louis

XVI had been beheaded, the new French government expected American support after it declared war on Great Britain and its European allies on February 1, 1793.

Great Britain, on the other hand, told the American government in no uncertain terms that any support for the French would be viewed as an act of war against itself. The United States was between a rock and a hard place.

Alexander Hamilton, in *The Federalist* No. 34, anticipated such a time. "Peace or war will not always be left to our option; that however moderate or unambitious we may be, we cannot count upon the moderation, or hope to extinguish the ambition of others." Thus, Hamilton always counseled naval and military preparedness, on the one hand, and restraint on the other.

The United States was not in a position to support either France or Great Britain, no matter how strongly each one pressured the new nation or its citizens. Only neutrality would serve American needs.

Alexander Hamilton believed that the United States was a "Hercules in the cradle." Years would pass before it had sufficient economic and military strength to challenge the European behemoths. As a result, he urged walking a neutral path while building up American military power.

Many thought that French and British meddling in American affairs sullied national honor. Most were partisan. They wanted to join one side or the other and, if necessary, participate in a foreign war. Hamilton disagreed.

"True honor is a rational thing," he wrote. "In most cases, it is consistent with honor to precede rupture by negotiation ... Honor cannot be wounded by consulting moderation." Thus, neutrality with both France and Great Britain was pursued, despite much popular opposition, especially from the pro-France faction. And the young Republic grew stronger as a result.

Alexander Hamilton learned two things as a young man during the Revolutionary War. The first was that the United States needed a regular army and navy in order to defend itself. The second lesson was this: Peace is always preferable to war and is nearly always possible.

John Marshall ranked Hamilton next to Washington, and with the judgment of their great chief justice Americans are wont to be content. But wherever he is placed, so long as the people of the United States form one nation, the name of Alexander Hamilton will be held in high and lasting honor, and even in the wreck of governments that noble intellect would still command the homage of men.

—**Henry Cabot Lodge,**
U.S. Senator and author of
***Alexander Hamilton*, 1898**

Chapter Thirty

WISDOM

———— ❧ ————

The truth is, in human affairs there is no good, pure and unmixed: every advantage has two sides: and wisdom consists in availing ourselves of the good, and guarding as much as possible against the bad.
      —**Alexander Hamilton,**
      letter to Robert Morris,
      April 30, 1781

Alexander Hamilton, while still in the Army, wrote a long letter to financier Robert Morris about what was needed to develop an American economy. Clearly the work of a deep thinker, the letter contains a remarkable gem. It is nothing less than one of Hamilton's guides for looking at a problem.

To summarize: (1) Nothing is purely good. (2) Every advantage has two sides. And (3) wisdom consists in identifying and holding on to the good while guarding

117

against that which is bad.

With a speed that astounded his peers, Alexander Hamilton was able to penetrate and dissect most issues. He avoided discussions of whether something was good or not. By his own admission, "there is no good, pure and unmixed."

Rather, he marshaled his energy in the direction of advantage—of realizing that there can be a larger benefit to some courses of action than to others. Furthermore, "Every advantage has two sides," Hamilton reasoned.

Not every problem was like the scenario Odysseus faced in the Odyssey, when he was forced to steer his ship between the rock Scylla and the whirlpool Charybdis (Hamilton used the images of Scylla and Charybdis more than once in his writings when talking about the need, sometimes, to navigate between twin and opposite dangers). In some situations, it's possible to select the best among several good options.

A careful study of Alexander Hamilton's thought reveals that he approached decision-making in a methodical way. He looked at all possible options, ranked them, and adopted the one that promised to be the best.

Hamilton hewed to that which is good while "guarding as much as possible against the bad." For him, decision-making was too important to be left up to whim and fancy.

Chapter Thirty-one

WORK

_____ ∼ _____

_It is a just observation, that minds of the strongest
and most active powers for their proper objects,
fall below mediocrity, and labour with effect, if
confined to uncongenial pursuits._
            —**Alexander Hamilton,**
            "Report on Manufactures,"
            December 5, 1791

Alexander Hamilton's capacity for work astounded
nearly everyone. At the age of 9, he began as a
clerk for the Saint Croix import/export firm of Beekman
and Cruger. At fourteen, when his employer absented
himself for several months, Hamilton directed all the
company's activities, dealing with attorneys, ship cap-
tains, and other merchants.

During his lifetime, Hamilton was a clerk, student,
soldier, lawyer, politician, journalist, entrepreneur, and

governmental official. He also established banks, a newspaper, and a manufacturing center.

Though he died at age 47, Hamilton left behind a larger body of written material than any other founding father. He also was an attentive husband and father to eight children (one was killed during the last years of his own life and an eighth was born soon thereafter).

An insight into Hamilton's prodigious labor is found in the above passage from his 1791 "Report on Manufactures." Sustained Herculean effort is possible when one enjoys the work itself or perhaps when one realizes the importance of doing particular tasks for the public good.

As Secretary of the Treasury, Alexander Hamilton was sometimes worn out having to meet the demands of Congress. Partisan politics forced him to generate reports that were otherwise unnecessary but always time consuming. He chafed under these demands but always met the deadline.

Alexander Hamilton believed that the work he undertook for the United States was important. Though it came at a great cost to his family and to his personal finances, Hamilton worked tirelessly on behalf of his adopted nation.

Yet not long after the death of his son Philip in 1801, in a duel, Hamilton, obviously depressed, questioned all that he had done. "Mine is an odd destiny," he wrote Gouverneur Morris. "Perhaps no man in the United States has sacrificed or done more for the present Constitution than myself; and contrary to all my anticipations of its fate, as you know from the very beginning, I am still labouring to prop the frail and worthless fabric. Yet I have the murmurs of its friends no less than the curses of its foes for my reward. What can I do better than withdraw from the scene? Every day proves to me more and more, that this American world was not made for me."

Of course, Hamilton did not "withdraw from the scene." He continued to write essays for the press and to propose new measures to "prop" the Constitution, laboring all the while in his private law practice.

Hard work was a lifelong habit for Alexander Hamilton. And nothing brought him greater pleasure than laboring tirelessly on behalf of his vision of the United States of America.

Hamilton, the most brilliant American statesman who ever lived, possessing the loftiest and keenest intellect of his time, was of course easily the foremost champion in the ranks of the New York Federalists; second to him came Jay, pure, strong, and healthy in heart, body, and mind. Both of them watched with uneasy alarm the rapid drift toward anarchy; and both put forth all their efforts to stem the tide. They were of course too great men to fall in with the views of those whose antagonism to tyranny made them averse from order. They had little sympathy with the violent prejudices produced by the war. In particular they abhorred the vindictive laws directed against the persons and properties of Tories; and they had the manliness to come forward as the defenders of the helpless and excessively unpopular Loyalists. They put a stop to the wrongs which were being inflicted on these men, and finally succeeded in having them restored to legal equality with other citizens, standing up with generous fearlessness against the clamor of the mob.

—Theodore Roosevelt,
26th President of the
United States

A CHRONOLOGY
OF ALEXANDER
HAMILTON'S LIFE

1757   January 11, born on the Island of Nevis in the British West Indies to James Hamilton and Rachel Faucett Lavien.

1765   Family moves to the Danish island of Saint Croix.

1766   James Hamilton (father) leaves family, never to return.

1766-68 Hamilton goes to work as a clerk for the merchant firm of Beekman and Cruger.

1768   February 19, Rachel Hamilton (mother) dies.

         Hamilton and older brother James live with Cousin Peter Lytton.

         Guardian Cousin Peter Lytton commits suicide within a year.

1772   Hamilton left in charge of firm when Nicholas Cruger goes to New York to regain health.

1773   After June 3, Hamilton leaves for mainland,

the 13 colonies.

Attends "prep" school in Elizabethtown, New Jersey.

December 16, Boston Tea Party occurs in Boston, Massachusetts.

Hamilton enters King's College (now Columbia University) late in 1773 or early in 1774.

1774   Hamilton writes his first public political piece upholding the Boston Tea Party as a necessary event.

July 6, Hamilton gives an impromptu speech at a public gathering of the Sons of Liberty, a secret society to fight oppression by British Parliament.

1775   April 18-19, Paul Revere's Midnight Ride and the Battle of Lexington, Massachusetts (the first military clash between British forces and the colonists).

Hamilton joins the "Corsicans" a New York militia company.

May 10, hundreds of protestors gather to tar and feather Dr. Cooper, the President of King's College and an ardent Tory. Hamilton gives impromptu speech on the stoop of Dr. Cooper's residence, delaying attackers and giving Cooper enough time to flee.

1776   Classes at King's College are suspended due to the war.

        March 14, Hamilton is appointed Captain of the Provincial Company of Artillery.

1777   March 1, appointed Aide-de-Camp to General Washington.

1780   December 14, marries Elizabeth Schuyler.

1781   April 30, resigns from Washington's staff.

        October 14, leads attack on Redoubt Number 10 at the Battle of Yorktown.

1782   July 22, admitted to practice law in New York.

1783   Treaty of Paris formally ends the Revolutionary War and recognizes the sovereignty of the colonies.

1784   John Jay and Hamilton help to re-open King's College under the name of Columbia College.

1786   September 14, delegate to Annapolis Convention which calls for Constitutional Convention.

1787   May 25-September 17, attends Constitutional Convention in Philadelphia.

        Writes *The Federalist* papers.

1789   September 11, appointed first Secretary of the Treasury.

1790   January 14, issues *Report on the Public Credit.*

June 21, Congress agrees to assume all Revolutionary War debts. Capitol to be located on Potomac River.

December, develops plan for a national bank.

1794   September 30, takes a leading role in suppressing the Whiskey Rebellion.

1795   January 31, resigns as Secretary of the Treasury.

1796   August 25, discloses Maria Reynolds affair.

1798   July 25, appointed Major General. Functions as Inspector General (Second in Command) of Army.

1800   June 2, retires from Army.

October, writes essay criticizing John Adams' presidential abilities. Adams is not re-elected.

1801   February 17, helps Thomas Jefferson win contested presidential election over Aaron Burr.

November 16, founds *New York Evening Post.*

November 23, Philip Hamilton, Hamilton's oldest son, killed in duel.

1802   April, proposes Christian Constitutional Society.

1804   July 11, mortally wounded in duel at Weehawken, New Jersey with Aaron Burr. Hamilton dies on July 12.

July 14, buried in Trinity Church graveyard in Manhattan, New York.

1854   November 9, Elizabeth Schuyler Hamilton dies.

CREDITS

Jacket illustration (color) and opposite title page (black and white):

John Trumbull, American, 1756-1843
Alexander Hamilton, 1806
Oil on canvas 77.79 x 62.55 cm (30⅝ x 24⅝ in.)
Museum of Fine Arts, Boston
Bequest of R. C. Winthrop 94.167
Photograph © May 2009 Museum of Fine Arts, Boston

Hamilton was fortunate that his wife spent the rest of her life collecting his letters from friends and colleagues. A number of collections of his papers exist. Most quotations in this book come from the versions edited by his son John C. Hamilton (7 volumes) and Henry Cabot Lodge (12 volumes). The quotations from Gouveneur Morris' eulogy are in William Coleman's collection of documents related to the death of Alexander Hamilton cited in the bibliography.

Some quotations come from *The Papers of Alexander Hamilton,* edited by Harold C. Syrett. Copyright © 1961, 1972, 1977, Columbia University Press. Reprinted with permission of the publisher are the quotations on pages 33, 59, 75 and 94 (the hurricane).

On page 20, the quotation from the John Dickinson letter is courtesy of the Historical Society of Pennsylvania (Logan Papers, Volume 12, page 84).

RECOMMENDED READING

For those who want to read about Alexander Hamilton, may I suggest the following:

~ *Alexander Hamilton, American* by Richard Brookhiser. This biography is in the tradition of the ancients such as Plutarch, who benefitted Hamilton greatly.

~ *www.HamiltonSpeaks.com.* This is my website and several of Hamilton's writings are on it. They are meaty and deserve concentrated attention and thought.

If you want to be more Hamiltonian, then I suggest you master the information in the following books:

~ *The 7 Habits of Highly Successful People* by Stephen R. Covey. Hamilton believed in working on your character. This book has a set method for doing just that.

~ *de Bono's Thinking Course* by Edward de Bono. Hamilton was a deep and systematic thinker. He would approve of anyone honing their thinking skills.

~ *The Thirteen American Arguments: Enduring Debates That Define and Inspire Our Country* by Howard Fineman. Our founders grappled with some of the same issues that face us today. This book gives a history of the ever-changing answers.

BIBLIOGRAPHY

Adair, Douglas and Marvin Harvey. "Was Alexander Hamilton a Christian Statesman?" *The William and Mary Quarterly 12*, no. 2, April 1955.

Adams, James Truslow, ed. *Hamiltonian Principles.* Boston: Little, Brown, 1928.

Ambrose, Douglas and Robert W.T. Martin, eds. *The Many Faces of Alexander Hamilton.* New York: New York University, 2006.

Brookhiser, Richard. *Alexander Hamilton, American.* New York: Free Press, 2003.

_____. *What Would the Founders Do? (Our Questions Their Answers).* New York: Basic Books, 2006.

Chernow, Ron. *Alexander Hamilton.* New York: Penguin Press, 2003.

Coleman, William. *A Collection of the Facts and Documents, Relative to the Death of Major-General Alexander Hamilton; With Comments: Together With the Various Orations, Sermons, and Eulogies, that Have Been Published Or Written on His Life and Character.* Boston: Houghton Mifflin, 1904.

Freeman, Joanne, ed. *Alexander Hamilton, Writings.* New York: Library of America, 2001.

Flexner, James Thomas. *The Young Hamilton*. Boston: Little, Brown, 1978.

Hamilton, Allan McLane. *The Intimate Life of Alexander Hamilton*. New York: Scribner's, 1910.

Hamilton, John C., ed. *The Works of Alexander Hamilton; Comprising His Correspondence, and His Political and Official Writings*, 7 vols. New York: Francis, 1851.

Harper, John Lamberton. *American Machiavelli, Alexander Hamilton and the Origins of U.S. Foreign Policy*. New York: Cambridge, 2004.

Hickey, Donald R. and Connie D. Clark, eds. *Citizen Hamilton, The Wit & Wisdom of an American Founder*. Lanham, Maryland: Rowman & Littlefield, 2006.

Johnson, Paul. *A History of the American People*. New York: HarperCollins, 1997.

Knott, Stephen F. *Alexander Hamilton and the Persistence of Myth*. Lawrence: University Press of Kansas, 2002.

Lodge, Henry Cabot. *Alexander Hamilton*. Boston: Houghton, Mifflin, 1898.

_____, ed. *The Works of Alexander Hamilton,* 12 vols. New York: Putnam's, 1904.

McDonald, Forrest. *Alexander Hamilton: A Biography*. New York: Norton, 1979.

Morris, Anne Cary, ed. *The Diary and Letters of Gou-veneur Morris,* 2 vols. New York: Scribner's, 1888.

Morris, Richard B., ed. *Alexander Hamilton and the Founding of the Nation.* New York: Dial, 1957.

Pontuso, James F. "The Case of Alexander Hamilton." *Perspectives on Political Science 22,* no. 2, Spring 1993.

Rhodehamel, John, ed. *George Washington, Writings.* New York: Library of America, 1997.

Schachner, Nathan. *Alexander Hamilton.* New York: Appleton-Century, 1946.

_____. "Alexander Hamilton Viewed by His Friends: The Narratives of Robert Troup and Hercules Mulligan." *The William and Mary Quarterly 4,* no. 2, April 1947.

Sparks, Jared. *The Life of Gouveneur Morris, with Selections from his Correspondence and Miscellaneous Papers,* 3 vols. Boston: Gray & Bowen, 1832.

Syrett, Harold C. *et al.,* eds. *The Papers of Alexander Hamilton,* 26 vols. New York: Columbia University Press, 1961-87.

INDEX

It seemed as if God had called him suddenly into existence, that he might assist to save a world!

—Gouveneur Morris, Eulogy at Hamilton's funeral by founding father and good friend

～

Chapter Twenty-five

These pages replace pages 97 to 100

SLAVERY

The only distinction between freedom and slavery consists in this: In the former state a man is governed by the laws to which he has given his consent, either in person, or by his representatives; in the latter, he is governed by the will of another. In the one case, his life and property are his own; in the other, they depend upon the pleasure of his master.

—**Alexander Hamilton,**
A Full Vindication of the
Measures of Congress,
December 15, 1774

When the Declaration of Independence was adopted by the Second Continental Congress on July 4, 1776, nearly half of those voting for it owned slaves. Clearly, the Declaration's lofty rhetoric, "we hold these truths to be self-evident, that all men are created equal," did not really apply to all men. This prompted one English observer to comment that those who yelped most about liberty also had whips in one hand to beat frightened slaves.

Of all those who rallied to the cause of liberty at that time, Alexander Hamilton was in a rather unique position when it came to slavery. Although he did not own slaves, he knew as much about the "peculiar institution," as it was called by some, as did any slave owner or trader. Hamilton's employer on the island of

Saint Croix, Nicholas Cruger, received at least one shipment of slaves from Africa while Hamilton was in his employ. The *Royal Danish American Gazette*, a local paper, announced on January 26, 1771, that Mr. Cruger, "of said Cruger's yard," was selling "300 prime slaves" in association with Nicholas Kortright.

Slavery was an overwhelming feature of life on Saint Croix. In 1773, according to poll-tax lists, Saint Croix had 24,126 inhabitants, including children under the age of twelve. Of these, 2,067 were white. That means that there were more than ten non-whites for every white person. To be sure, some of the non-whites were free. But the great majority lived in slavery. The aforementioned *Gazette*, during the time of Hamilton's residency, is filled with notices of slave auctions and advertisements offering rewards for runaway slaves.

A fourteen or fifteen year-old clerk on the Island of Saint Croix probably didn't have many options when it came to making a living. Hamilton may not have wanted anything to do with slavery. But the truth of the matter is that Alexander Hamilton was involved in the slave trade. His employer engaged in it, and Hamilton's education in New York, undertaken by some island residents, was financed by crops grown using slave labor.

What did Hamilton think about slavery? The essay quoted at the beginning of this chapter, written at the beginning of the American Revolution to explain why the colonists must separate from Great Britain, makes it clear. Hamilton was under no illusions about slavery. A slave "is governed by the will of another," he writes.

But unlike many founding fathers, Alexander Hamilton did not make an easy peace with slavery. During the Revolutionary War, Hamilton and his friend John Laurens proposed raising "three or four battalions of negroes." Explaining the plan to John Jay, Hamilton notes, "The contempt we have been taught to entertain for the blacks, makes us fancy many things that are founded neither in reason nor experience."

Their "natural faculties are probably as good as ours," Hamilton reckoned. They will make excellent soldiers and, if anything, because of the "habit of subordination" they are obliged to "acquire from a life of servitude," they will require less time to train than their white counterparts.

Not surprisingly, the plan to raise African-American battalions went nowhere. But soon after the war, in 1785, Alexander Hamilton became a founding member of the New York Society for Promoting the Manumission of Slaves. In addition, he became a member of a steering committee "to Report a Line of Conduct to be recommended."

The line of conduct taken was this: On March 13, 1786, Hamilton was one of those who signed a petition addressed to the New York Legislature urging the end of the slave trade. It was, the petition said, a horrid commerce, "repugnant to humanity." A free and enlightened people must never sanction something so "inconsistent with liberality and justice."

Like many Americans, Alexander Hamilton was implicated in the institution of slavery. Unlike most of them, he publicly spoke against it and pledged himself to end it.